KAFKA AND LANGUAGE

STUDIES IN AUSTRIAN LITERATURE, CULTURE, AND THOUGHT

GABRIELE VON NATZMER COOPER

KAFKA AND LANGUAGE

IN THE STREAM OF

THOUGHTS AND LIFE

ARIADNE PRESS

Library of Congress Cataloging-in-Publication Data

Cooper, Gabriele von Natzmer
    Kafka and language: in the stream of thoughts and life /
    Gabriele von Natzmer Cooper.
        p. cm. --(Studies in Austrian literature, culture, and thought)
    Includes bibliographical references (p.   ) and index.
    ISBN 0-929497-38-4.
    1. Kafka, Franz, 1883-1924--Knowledge--Language and languages.
2. Kafka, Franz, 1883-1924--Language. 3. Kafka, Franz, 1883-1924
--Aesthetics. I. Title. II. Series.
PT2621.A26Z6635 1991
833'.912--dc20   91-2360
                                            CIP

Cover: Art Director: George McGinnes; Designer: Gary Kent Jackson

This book was typeset by Gerhard Obenaus with a Hewlitt Packard LaserJet III

Nur in dem Fluß der Gedanken und des Lebens haben die Worte Bedeutung.

Ludwid Wittgenstein

Acknowledgment

I wish to thank James W. Marchand and Peter Winch for the patience and understanding with which they guided me toward the completion of this study. I also wish to thank Randy Cooper, Bruce Goldberg, and the members of the Wittgenstein Discussion Group for their many illuminating contributions. Finally, I want to thank my editors who, after all, made this book possible.

To Randy, Claus, David and Gabi

Abbreviations

A	Kafka, *Amtliche Schriften*
B	Kafka, *Beschreibung eines Kampfes.* *Die zwei Fassungen. Parallelausgabe*
Br	Kafka, *Briefe*
DVS	*Deutsche Vierteljahrsschrift*
E	Kafka, *Erzählungen*
F	Kafka, *Briefe an Felice*
GRM	*Germanisch-Romanische Monatsschrift*
H	Kafka, *Hochzeitsvorbereitungen auf dem Lande und andere Prosa aus dem Nachlaß*
HS W	Heine, *Sämtliche Werke*
Jb. d. DSG	*Jahrbuch der deutschen Schillergesellschaft*
KW	Kraus, *Werke*
M	Kafka, *Briefe an Milena*
MLR	*Modern Language Review*
O	Kafka, *Briefe an Ottla*
R	Kafka, *Romane*
SSW	Storm, *Sämtliche Werke*
T	Kafka, *Tagebücher*
WA	Wittgenstein, *Lectures and Conversations on Aesthetics, Psychology and Religious Belief*
WB	Wittgenstein, *Briefe an Ludwig Ficker*
WCV	Wittgenstein, *Culture and Value*
WE	Wittgenstein, *Lecture on Ethics*
WPI	Wittgenstein, *Philosophical Investigations*
WZ	Wittgenstein, *Zettel*
ZDP	*Zeitschrift für deutsche Philologie*

Table of Contents

Introduction

In the following I try to explore what is often referred to as the crisis of language in modern literature by applying to this problem Ludwig Wittgenstein's insights into the nature of language. While only the last chapter will be taken up by a discussion of philosophical considerations, for the purpose of the introduction these considerations have to be discussed in some detail to make intelligible the argument on which the book is based.

Ludwig Wittgenstein began thinking about language from the point of view of a logician, trying to work out the logical conditions required by a system of signs referring to the world. He arrived at what he considered the only possible account of such a system but had second thoughts on the matter over a period of years. It was then that he fully developed his major ideas about language. Whereas he had previously thought that language represented the world by following fixed rules of logic, he now came to see that no hidden logical structure could exist in language and, more importantly, that such a structure was not required to make words meaningful. Language, he realized, connects with the world not through logic but through human action. Our words derive their sense from their context, i.e., the life of the people who use them, their ways of acting and reacting, their perceptions of the world, their feelings, their culture, etc. Words do not have meaning by referring to the world, but rather by playing a certain role in human life and action.

Wittgenstein's thoughts about the nature of language can, I believe, give us an entirely new way of looking at one of the most troubling problems of modern literature, the so-called phenomenon of "speechlessness," i.e., the misgivings about language among twentieth-century writers, resulting in some cases in a complete breakdown of creativity, literal "speechlessness." Complaints about the inadequacy of language have been voiced in previous centuries but never before, it seems, with such vehemence and such grave consequences for artistic productivity. Poetic "speechlessness" represents a striking and ominous cultural phenomenon. Most studies of this subject are based on the kinds of linguistic theories Wittgenstein came to reject, i.e., theories that consider language as essentially symbolic and descriptive and that have as their logical conclusion some form of skepticism, as represented, for example, by the Austrian writer and philosopher Fritz Mauthner. Mauthner's *Beiträge zu einer Kritik der Sprache* appeared in 1901, the same year in which Hugo von Hofmannsthal published his famous "Ein Brief," formulating doubts about language that seemed so similar to his own that Mauthner assumed they had been inspired by his book. The influence of this philosophically founded skepticism was not limited to German-speaking countries. James Joyce, for example, loved Mauthner's book and had Samuel Beckett read it to him. In fact many literary works have since been written that seem affected by a Mauthnerian kind of skepticism, and one might well conclude that this philosophical view has helped to shape the character of modern literature.

However, if the descriptive account of language is as fundamentally misguided as Wittgenstein felt it was, the modern literary crisis cannot simply be explained in terms of the realization on the part of writers that our words are basically inadequate. Philosophical considerations may play a part in some ways, but there are a variety of other factors that contribute far more importantly, and these factors will differ from case to case. In my book, therefore, I examine the relationship of one particular author, Franz Kafka, to his medium, without basing my analysis on the descriptive-symbolic theory of language. Language, says Wittgenstein, is a form of life. It has meaning only in the stream of human activity. If we are to understand the problems in twentieth-century literature with respect to language, rather than resorting to linguistic theories, we must turn to the individual writers, their lives, their views of themselves as artists and human beings, their feelings about the world, their work methods, their standards and goals, the standards and goals of their culture, etc. It is only in this living context that their attitudes toward art and language can become intelligible.

I will focus my investigations on Kafka, whose difficulties with writing are particularly well-documented in his diaries and letters. Unlike Hofmannsthal, whose professed skepticism toward language did not seem to interfere significantly with his productivity, Kafka belonged to those writers for whom the creative process became extremely problematic. None of his novels was ever completed. His diaries are full of fragmentary beginnings of stories. He excelled in short prose pieces but considered so few of them acceptable that his publisher had to resort to using an unusually large print in order to give his first book a respectable size. As a result of the halting, continuously interrupted flow of his work, his recurring crises and growing self-doubts, he left behind only a limited oeuvre.

Throughout Kafka's writings there occur remarks about language, art and aesthetics. While some of them express a skeptical attitude towards his medium, others indicate great faith in the power of words. His relation to language was complicated and cannot be appreciated without taking into account such diverse factors as the linguistic conditions under which he grew up in Prague, his love-hate relationship with German literature, his awareness of Judaism, his fondness for eastern European Jewry and the Yiddish theater, his fascination with ordinary conversations between the people around him, his passion for reading aloud and the metaphors he used to describe language. When seen in this context, his difficulties with writing can no longer be explained simply as a result of theoretical skepticism. Such an explanation would not do justice to the complexity of this writer, his view of himself and of his relation to his culture.

The first chapter presents Kafka's linguistic environment and his aesthetic and emotional responses to spoken language. While his at times whimsical descriptions of verbal utterances contain an amazing wealth of imagery, they also emphasize his personal isolation and his great difficulties in talking to others. Writing and reading literature became his substitute for human contact. The times he felt most at home with spoken language are perhaps when he read aloud from literary works. The second chapter focuses on his sense of cultural alienation manifested by his involvement with the Yiddish theater and its language, through which, for a while, he hoped to find his spiritual roots. The third chapter examines his relationship to German literature, which was dominated for him by the standards of Goethe's language, and from which he saw himself excluded in an almost metaphysical way. The fourth chapter deals with his aesthetic ideals of purity and spontaneity that grew out of his visionary, meditative method of writing, and his difficulties in achieving these ideals due to the continuous conflict between his artistic and his professional work. The fifth and final chapter discusses Kafka's explicit statements about the limitations of language, interpreting them not, as has been done before, in a skeptical sense, but rather in the sense of the last sentence of Wittgenstein's *Tractatus*. Certain aspects of human experience are quite beyond the power of discursive language.

Kafka's problems with language expressed themselves in a variety of ways. He found it difficult to have conversations with people, yet "a true word from person to person" was the thing he cherished most. The German he spoke had, because he felt so keenly that it was an adopted language, no warmth for him, yet he longed to make it come alive in the sentences of his stories. And when he wanted to express his religious thoughts, he found that all that mattered could, if at all, only be said in pictures. Yet he continued writing until a few weeks before his death.

1

"Das Temperament der Sprache"
Kafka's Love of Language

Both the complex linguistic situation in which Kafka grew up, and the role language played in his personal life must be looked at before his relationship to the language of literature can be described, for the biographical conditions form the basis on which that relationship eventually developed.[1] Other relevant details have to be brought out too, such as his fondness for reading aloud, his metaphoric descriptions of language, his fascination with gestures and speech mannerisms. For it is these kinds of details that are needed in order for us to describe with some validity Kafka's relationship to language. The purpose of this chapter is to paint a sort of panoramic picture of language in Kafka's life. It will be divided into four parts, each focusing on a particular feature of this picture, the first dealing with the linguistic situation of Prague, the second with Kafka's manner of reading aloud, the third with the way he wrote about language, and the fourth with the significance that human conversation assumed for him.

I

In 1920 Kafka spent three months in Meran to improve his health. Three years earlier he had been diagnosed for tuberculosis. In spite of his attempts to cure himself through rest and a healthy life (he moved into the country to stay with his youngest and favorite sister Ottla) he had grown increasingly worse. He may have considered his three months in Meran his last chance to get well, because when they were over he told Max Brod in a letter: "Nur eine Stelle stört an Deinem Brief. Wo Du vom Gesund-werden sprichst. Nein, davon ist seit einem Monat keine Rede mehr" (Br 276). He continued his treatments patiently but without conviction and observed his fellow guests at the *Pension Ottoburg*, with whom he developed a peculiar relationship. He described this relationship in two letters to Brod. His description is worth a closer look, for it highlights two aspects of his life that played a central role in his relationship to language: First, his peculiar German accent, which marked him as a "Deutschböhme" and points toward the problematic linguistic situation in which he grew up. And second, his personal shyness, which at times made human contact excruciatingly difficult for him, so that he preferred most of his life to communicate with others through letters (Br 270 f., 274 f.).

Initially he represents to the guests of the *Ottoburg*, who are all "ganz deutsch-christlich" a great puzzlement, because they cannot place his accent:

Nach den ersten Worten kam hervor, daß ich aus Prag bin; beide, der General (dem ich gegenübersaß) und der Oberst kannten Prag. Ein Tscheche? Nein. Erkläre nun diesen treuen deutschen militärischen Augen was du eigentlich bist. Irgendwer sagt "Deutschböhme," ein anderer "Kleinseite." Dann legt sich das Ganze und man ißt weiter, aber der General

mit seinem scharfen, im österreichischen Heer philo-
logisch geschulten Ohr, ist nicht zufrieden, nach dem
Essen fängt er wieder den Klang meines Deutsch zu
bezweifeln an, vielleicht zweifelt übrigens mehr das
Auge als das Ohr. Nun kann ich das mit meinem Judentum zu erklären versuchen. Wissenschaftlich ist er
jetzt zufrieden gestellt, aber menschlich nicht. . . .
Menschlich befriedigt mich ja das auch nicht sehr,
warum muß ich sie quälen? (Br 270 f.)

The acute uneasiness and the sense of social illegitimacy
generated in Kafka by this episode is somewhat reminiscent
of Thomas Mann's figure of the artist Tonio Kröger, who
grows up "allein und ausgeschlossen von den Ordentlichen
und Gewöhnlichen"[2] and is almost arrested when after years
of absence he returns as a stranger to his north German
hometown because it is difficult to place him "hierarchisch
und bürgerlich."[3]   Like Tonio, Kafka had an unusually dark
complexion and this, combined with his strange Prague
accent, made him something of a social oddity and thus an
uncomfortable outsider in the *Ottoburg*.   For the famous
"Prager Deutsch," the German spoken by the (in a large part
Jewish) intellectuals and artists of Prague, had very
distinctive qualities (cf. Wagenbach 1958, 75).[4]

Egon Kisch (1885-1948) has written a marvelous description of the German spoken in Prague at Kafka's time.[5]
According to Kisch all soft stops (b, d, g) were pronounced
hard, all hard stops (p, t, k), soft, i.e., "b" as "p" as in "ich
pin" or "k" as "g" as in "gleine Kretl."[6]   It is unlikely that
Kafka's German displayed some of the more extreme features
described by Kisch, such as stressing the first syllable of all
words, even if that syllable was merely a prefix, but one can
safely assume that his pronunciation did have a great deal of
the distinct coloring of the "Kleinseitner Deutsch" as the
Prague German was sometimes called, such as, for example,

the "lack of rounded and mixed vowels."[7] ("Kleinseite" was the name of a western section of the city.) Pavel Trost maintains that the "Kleinseitner Deutsch" was spoken by the "Kleinbürgertum," i.e., predominantly by bilingual Czechs but never by the "Prager Schmock," and was quite distinct from the highly educated German spoken by the circles in which Kafka moved. Kafka, after all, spoke the kind of correct and pure German that gave rise to the century-old notion of a perfect Prague high German.[8] Whatever his problems with German were, they did not in any serious way concern proper usage. Nor is it entirely accurate to speak of an impoverishment of Kafka's language (cf. Wagenbach 1958, 85, 94).[9] That there are only few and general adjectives in his prose,[10] does not necessarily represent an impoverishment of language, just as the simple brush strokes of a Zen drawing do not imply an impoverishment of painting techniques.   It seems therefore somewhat misleading to explain this feature of Kafka's style as a result of Prague German "Wortschwund," as Wagenbach appears to do (Wagenbach 1958, 85).

The German-speaking population of Prague in 1900, representing roughly 10% of the city's total population, had developed a rich and intensive cultural life (cf. Wagenbach 1958, 71).[11] As Kisch reports, the German-speaking population possessed two "prunkvolle" theaters, a huge concert hall, two universities, five *Gymnasien* (humanistic high schools that taught primarily classical languages) and four *Oberrealschulen* (high schools teaching sciences and modern languages),[12] two daily papers, several large assembly halls and an "active social life."[13] The majority of this population consisted according to Kisch of "Großbürger," i.e., wealthy businessmen, manufacturers, entrepreneurs, bankers, but also university professors, higher ranking officers and state officials.[14]   And perhaps as much as two thirds of this cultivated German-speaking upper class was Jewish (cf.

Wagenbach 1958, 75, 206).[15]

This was the world in which Kafka grew up.[16] But he did not quite belong to it, for his father had only recently established himself in the upper-middle class (cf. Wagenbach 1958, 19 f.). Hermann Kafka spoke Czech and during his first years in Prague managed to pass as Czech, thus being spared anti-Semitic assaults from the Czech populace (Wagenbach 1958, 20). However, he chose to give up this protection, as Wagenbach says, for the sake of joining the German-speaking upper-middle class of Prague (Wagenbach 1958, 20). As the few postcards by him that have been preserved show, his German was very poor (Wagenbach 1958, 194). This is also indicated by the fact that Kafka gave him the Czech rather than the German translation of Benjamin Franklin's autobiography (Wagenbach 1958, 194). Kafka dedicated his collection of stories *Der Landarzt* to his father (Br 228), but in his "Brief an den Vater" he talks about his father's disapproving attitude toward his writing, which the older Kafka no doubt considered a "breadless art" and therefore useless. It was a family joke that Kafka's father would greet his books with "Legs auf den Nachttisch!" (H 203). Hermann Kafka took a dim view of his son's artistic inclinations, because as a man who had worked his way out of severest poverty, a fact that naturally formed his entire outlook on life, he had neither the wisdom nor the education to appreciate these inclinations. But it is quite possible that it was also his poor German that made him reluctant to read his son's stories.

One can assume that the father spoke Czech at home most of the time (cf., e.g., Br 249). His special protégée among the household staff was Fräulein Werner, who spoke only Czech and was in charge of Kafka's (much younger) sisters (cf. Wagenbach 1958, 26). This woman, called by everyone simply "slečna" (Miss) taught Kafka Czech (Wagenbach 1958, 26). Although his knowledge of Czech must have been good enough to satisfy any school requirements, he later took Czech in high school, partly, perhaps, because at that time his father still had hopes that the son would some day join his business, which used primarily Czech-speaking employees, and partly also because Kafka himself may have wished to improve his knowledge of the language spoken by the majority of the people he encountered in his daily life. As he himself once remarked in his diary, he spoke Czech quite fluently, using it, for example, to persuade one of his father's ex-employees not to claim any insurance benefits (T 175). Many years later, he assured Milena Jesenská, who had just translated his story "Der Heizer" into Czech, that he too had a "Sprachgefühl" (M 22) for this language and could appreciate its "Sprachmusik" (M 28). But toward the end of his life he asked his Czech brother-in-law to translate an important official letter into Czech for him, indicating that he never was quite as much at ease with Czech as he was with German (O 147 f.).

As one reads Brod's and Wagenbach's descriptions of Kafka's early childhood, i.e., the time that he learned German so that at six he could attend a German school, one wonders who taught him. His mother, who, unlike her husband, came from a wealthy family and had been raised speaking German (Wagenbach 1958, 22), had to help her husband in his business and could not spend much time with her son (Wagenbach 1958, 25 f.). There was a German-speaking "Kinderfräulein" who would in later years come to visit Kafka (cf. T 169 f.). There also was a somewhat sadistic cook who took him to school once he was old enough and threatened (in German) to disclose his bad behavior at home to the teacher (cf. M 64). On the way, they passed a Czech grade school with a sign over the door that said: "A Czech child belongs in a Czech school" (Wagenbach 1958, 29), reminding the little boy that even though his father spoke Czech, he himself was not a Czech child. The complexity of the linguistic situation Kafka grew up in is perhaps best captured by Felix Weltsch's description of the elementary schools he and Kafka attended. There, according to Weltsch Czech Catholic clergymen taught German to children who came almost exclusively from Jewish families.[17]

Much is made of Kafka's uncertainty with respect to the use of the preposition "bis," which had acquired the sense of"wenn" or"sobald" in Prague German (cf. F 81; Br 169, 180 and 216; Wagenbach 1958, 90). As Max Brod notes, there are a few other distinctly Prague-flavored idioms in Kafka's writing: "beiläufig" instead of "ungefähr" or "einigermaßen," "an etwas vergessen" instead of "vergessen" and "wieso kommt es" instead of "wie kommt es" (F 81). As Brod notes, Karl Kraus published commentaries on these linguistic idiosyncrasies in his *Fackel* in 1921, for they were not restricted to Prague, but represented a Viennese phenomenon as well (F 81, Footnote 1).

It is, by the way, interesting that Kraus does not describe these "aberrations" as the result of missing "Sprachgefühl." The cases of "bis" (in the sense of "when") and "wieso kommt es," he feels, are simply a matter of conceptual confusion, but "vergessen an" has potential, could "work" given the right conditions: "Wie immer im Bereich der Sprache, wo die Gestaltung nicht von der Regel, sondern vom schöpferischen Willen bedingt ist, käme es hier durchaus auf die Kraft an, die die Sphäre durchdringt, in der das Vergessen sich begibt, auf den Atem des Satzes, auf die Umgebung der Anomalie, um sie glaubwürdig erscheinen zu lassen" (KW II 27). Kraus' point is important for our understanding of the true nature of Kafka's problem with Prague German. This problem was not that he had an inadequate command over the German language or lacked the genius to make this language work for him in spite of its local coloring. The fact that he used certain phrases that were idiomatic only in some parts of the Austro-Hungarian

Empire, would not, by itself, constitute a lack of German "Sprachgefühl." Such regional variances from the norms of proper high German would not really justify, for example, Wagenbach's claim that Kafka did not possess an "ursprünglich sicheres Sprachgefühl." As Richard Thieberger correctly points out, no German writer was given high German in his cradle.[18] That Kafka had to learn the correct high German use of "bis" at a rather late point in his life, is neither the sign nor the cause of a lacking feeling for the German language.

Yet Wagenbach's remark points to an important problem that arose for Kafka because of the conditions under which he learned German, a problem not so much the result of an inadequate command of the language, but rather the result of a certain stiltedness and sterility of Prague German, its "gewählter, gesuchter, geblümter Stil."[19] This sterility was first noted by Eisner: "How in the world should the inmate of a Prague Jewish-German ghetto know how the real people speak German . . . ?"[20] It is usually blamed on the isolated situation of the German-speaking Prague population surrounded like an island by the sea of the Czech population (cf. Wagenbach 1958, 80).[21] However, there was another feature of the Prague situation, a feature closely connected with its geographic and social isolation, but worth being singled out here, that seems to have lain at the very heart of the peculiar sterility of Prague German, i.e., the fact that most of its speakers belonged to the same section of the well-educated upper-middle class of that city. Everybody's language had been acquired in the same upper-middle-class households and schools, reflected the same upper-middle-class level of higher education and culture. There were no large German-speaking working-class areas, where, over the years, anything like an original Prague German dialect could have developed. There were none of the subcultures that are usually present in a linguistic community to give life to its language with their individualistic, often colorful adaptations. Kafka and his friends, it seems, never used any kind of special jargon, as most young people do, but were already communicating in high school through "gewählte, gesuchte, geblümte" sentences. It was precisely the absence of any vernacular or dialect that constituted the Prague language problem for Fritz Mauthner.

Mauthner, who spent his school years in Prague around the middle of the nineteenth century, traced his philosophical interest in language back to having grown up understanding three languages, German, "die Sprache der Beamten, der Bildung, der Dichtung," Czech, "die Sprache der Bauern und der Dienstmädchen" and some Hebrew, which formed the basis of the "Mauscheldeutsch," which as a child he heard from "Trödeljuden, aber gelegentlich auch von ganz gut gekleideten jüdischen Kaufleuten seines Umgangs oder gar seiner Verwandtschaft."[22] His artistic failure (he spent many years supporting himself by writing second-rate novels, and never, in any of his works, transcended a certain journalistic quality),[23] Mauthner explained by the absence of any dialect in the Prague German: " . . . für die Wortkunst fehlte mir das lebendige Wort einer eigenen Mundart."[24]

Mauthner's description of his youthful despair over not speaking a dialect relates directly to Kafka's central problem with the language of his art, German. As will be shown in my second and third chapters, this problem was expressed in almost identical terms by Kafka, for he too felt that in the German language "only dialects and the most personal high German" were alive (Br 337). The full force of this statement is brought out through the intense sense of loss expressed by Mauthner because he possessed neither a dialect nor the "most personal high German": " . . . ich besitze in meinem innern Sprachleben nicht die Kraft und die Schönheit einer Mundart. Und wenn jemand mir zuriefe: ohne Mundart sei man nicht im Besitze einer eigentlichen Muttersprache—so könnte ich vielleicht heute noch aufheulen, wie in meiner Jugend, aber ich könnte ihn nicht Lügen strafen. . . . Der Deutsche im Inneren von Böhmen . . . spricht ein papierenes Deutsch. . . . Es mangelt an Fülle des erdgewachsenen Ausdrucks, es mangelt an Fülle der mundartlichen Formen. Die Sprache ist arm. Und mit der Fülle der Mundart ist auch die Melodie der Mundart verloren gegangen."[25] The absence of any forms of dialect, i.e., forms of the German language that had been shaped through centuries of local use, adapting to the people speaking it and to their life-style, made the Prague German as rootless and detached from earth as Kafka saw himself when he complained that nothing he wrote came "from the root" (T 12). How can one hold on to a blade of grass that only starts growing in the middle of the stem, Kafka asked, capturing in this image the essence of Prague German (T 12).

When we talk of Prague German, we are not merely referring to language as it might be captured by rules of grammar and a dictionary, but rather to a society, a life-style, a literature and much more, all of which was characterized by a certain lack of cultural direction, an unsureness about one's spiritual and artistic goals. Kafka was extremely sensitive to the precarious situation of his culture, for he felt it was very much his own. He compared his situation to that of a Japanese acrobat performing his moves on a ladder that was resting in midair (T 12). Other writers in Prague shared the uncertainty of the cultural ground they stood on, but not all were as keenly aware of it. Wagenbach, noting this uncertainty, describes one of its tangible manifestations, the tendency of the "Prague Circle,"[26] the young writers who were Kafka's contemporaries, and for the most part his friends as well, toward purple prose and "Schwulst," "Geschmacklosigkeit und fragwürdige Vergleiche" (Wagenbach 1958, 82; cf. also 85 f.). Wagenbach also points out Kafka's remarkable achievement in completely abandoning the direction of such a self-conscious and artificial style (which he had initially adopted to some extent) in favor of a simple, clear, pure prose (cf. Wagenbach 1958, 87 ff.).

It is significant that Kurt Tucholsky (1890-1935) called Kafka's style "the best classical German of our time,"[27] for the ideal of classical German literature, epitomized by Goethe's "Urkraft" (Brod 1962, 151), still loomed large behind all the efforts of the young literati of Prague. But this ideal also played an important role in Vienna, where Kraus published his *Fackel* in defense of Goethe's language, as well as in Berlin, where Tucholsky was writing. And in this sense Max Brod is correct to protest against the view (taken by Eisner, Politzer, Wagenbach) that the situation of the "Prague Circle" was "unnaturally isolated" (Brod, *Prager Kreis* 151). Just as Viennese German speakers shared some of the idiosyncrasies of Prague German, the Viennese literary scene had much in common with that of Prague, and even of Berlin. Kraus' ghastly caricature of this literary scene in his "magische Operette" *Literatur oder man wird doch da sehen* specifically depicted German-speaking Jewish intellectuals of the Austro-Hungarian Empire, but was probably a fairly accurate representation of those of Germany as well (KW XIV 7-74).

It was this play that gave rise to Kafka's famous letter to Max Brod about the "Zigeunerliteratur" produced by the German-Jewish writers of his time. Kafka found Kraus' play "außerordentlich treffend, ins Herz treffend" because it touched on a problem that was not restricted to certain cities but was true of the entire "little world of German-Jewish literature," to which Kraus and Tucholsky belonged as well (Br 336). So it would be somewhat misleading to trace the stylistic awkwardness and uncertainty of the German-Jewish Prague writers exclusively back to their special linguistic situation (as Wagenbach does). For there are more universal factors, involving the complex history of the German-Jewish culture, that played an important part in the artistic problems of the "Prague Circle." I will discuss them in detail in the third chapter of this study.

II

Problems with language arose for Kafka from the outset of his life because he belonged to the small German-speaking subculture of Prague. Further—as will be discussed in the third chapter—he had to confront the difficult and troubling situation of those members of the German-speaking Jewry who, while participating most vigorously in the German culture, for a variety of reasons could not feel part of it. The profound effect *these* problems had on Kafka's life did not involve any philosophical considerations or linguistic theories, yet they may well have represented the single most important factor shaping his relationship to language. A discussion of this relationship, therefore, cannot, as it were, reach the heart of the matter by implying some kind of theory about language on the part of Kafka, as suggested, for example, by Anthony Thorlby or Susanne Kessler.[28] Kafka's problems with language were not based on any theoretical views he might have formed as he grew up, but arose, instead, out of the actual conditions of the world he lived in. Presenting these problems exclusively in terms of philosophical concepts, therefore, is misleading and distorts their character.

It would be equally misleading and distorting to present Kafka's relationship to language as one of skepticism, distrust and rejection.[29] Such a picture would leave out some of the most important features of that relationship, features that have a great deal of bearing on our understanding of his work. We must therefore include in this picture its very positive, emotionally satisfying dimension, i.e., his great love for language. He expressed this love in many ways but perhaps most poignantly in his passion for reading aloud.

As his diaries show, Kafka participated vigorously in the very active intellectual and cultural life of the "Prague Circle" for a number of years, attending numerous lectures, recitals, political meetings, concerts and plays. There were also regular weekly gatherings of the "inner Prague Circle" (Brod, *Prager Kreis* 120 f.), to which Kafka, Brod, Felix Weltsch and Oskar Baum belonged, and where the friends (all writers, Weltsch the most philosophically inclined) read aloud from their works and discussed them.   Reading literature aloud was an essential part of Kafka's relationship to language, for he loved to do it and, according to Brod, did it extremely well (cf. Brod 1962, 217). It is important to remember that Kafka's sentences, distinguished, as Brod says, by their "big long breath" (Brod 1962, 227), were always written with their spoken dimension in mind, and that all literature was for him an art form that required the human voice for its full unfolding.   Kafka's passion for reading aloud should not be disregarded in the context of discussing his problems with language, for it is a measure of the depth of his involvement with his art and therefore a measure, too, of the intensity of his feelings about language.

He himself has given us a detailed picture of the way he read aloud, for his diaries and letters contain many remarks about this great love of his (T 131, 181, 230, 282, 297, 305, 341, 460; Br 38, 213; F 155). As he confessed to Felice Bauer, he read "höllisch gern," for shouting into "vorberei-tete und aufmerksame Ohren . . . tut dem armen Herz so wohl" (F 155). Using a characteristically concrete image, he compares the pleasure of reading aloud a certain story to the pleasure of drawing a "Bindfaden" across his tongue (T 131). The following passage describes in detail the liberat-ing, self-asserting experience that reading aloud could be for Kafka: "Wie ich letzthin meinen Schwestern die Selbstbio-

graphie Mörikes vorlas, schon gut anfing, aber noch besser
fortsetzte und schließlich, die Fingerspitzen aufeinander
gelegt, mit meiner ruhig bleibenden Stimme innere Hindernis-
se bezwang, einen immer mehr sich ausbreitenden Ausblick
meiner Stimme verschaffte und schließlich das ganze Zimmer
rings um mich nichts anderes aufnehmen durfte als meine
Stimme" (T 181). With typical self-derision, he claimed that
the true motive behind his passion for reading aloud great
works of literature (such as Heinrich von Kleist's "Michael
Kohlhaas," which he read numerous times, once even at a
public recital), was only to achieve a "vain, false feeling of
unity" with the work and thus participate illegitimately in "all
the influence" it had exercised on his listeners (T 230 f.).
However, as emerges from one of Brod's accounts, Kafka
enjoyed his readings immensely and was far better at them
than the rather self-deprecating entry of January 4, 1912
indicates.

Discussing Kafka's literary taste and the works that had
the greatest influence on him as a writer, Brod mentions a
small collection of Chinese poems translated into German
prose by Hans Heilmann (cf. Brod 1959, 67 ff.).[30] According to Brod Kafka was extremely fond of this book, at times
even "preferred it to all others," and often read from it to his
friend (Brod 1959, 68). It is easy to see why Kafka found its
poems appealing. While they are translated into simple prose
sentences, these poems contain a wealth of pictures, representing through concrete situations of human life universal
human experiences and feelings, such as the loneliness of a
bride left behind by her new warrior husband, or the anger
of a woman ignored until late into the night by her scholarly
lover. Kafka's own writing might be characterized in this
way, for it too represents in clear and simple language very
concrete pictures of human beings, pictures that, in a sense,
have to speak for themselves. The image of Gregor Samsa
waking up as an insect represents such a picture. What could

be added to make more eloquent the vision of Gregor's many "pathetically thin" legs wiggling helplessly before his eyes (E 39)? Pictures and gestures represented the building blocks of Kafka's artistic language (to be discussed in the last two chapters). His literary taste and preference favored the concrete image and the expressive gesture. When he read aloud he submerged himself in the expressive dimension of language, its world of pictures and gestures.

As Brod reports, his friend accompanied his reading of the Chinese poems with vivid gestures and play-acting, dramatizing their words "mimisch mit unvergleichlich theatralischer Naivität." Sometimes, they would make Kafka chuckle, and at other times, they would bring him close to tears (Brod 1959, 68). One of the poems, addressed to a famous Chinese poet who had been given the name "Unerschöpflicher Tropfenfall" by his admirers, moved Kafka more than any other. The poet is described as letting the "tears of his soul" rain on his paper through his brush strokes, and it closes with the line "Und wenn das Lied vollendet ist, hört man um dich herum das bewundernde Murmeln unsterblicher Geister."[31] Brod comments: "Diese Zeile von Kafka gesprochen, klingt mir heute noch im Ohr; man sah, wenn er sie mit tiefer Stimme, langsam, feierlich die Hand hebend, dabei ganz heiter aussprach, die Genien rings um den Dichter sitzen und ihn anstaunen" (Brod 1959, 69). Brod's description conjures up a very different image of Kafka from the one he has acquired over the years among his readers as the author of "tragedies of loneliness, of hermetic isolation, of the curse of existence."[32]

Dark, even sinister elements undoubtedly pervade Kafka's stories. But we would not capture the spirit in which these stories were written by describing them in such terms alone. Because it is important for the purpose of this study to revaluate Kafka's attitude towards language and human life (for the two are intimately connected with each other), the spirit of his stories, particularly as expressed through his humor, will be discussed here in some detail. These stories often have the quality of nightmares, and yet at the same time they contain much of the playful humor and affectionate irony that manifested themselves so strikingly in Kafka's theatrical manner of reading the Chinese poems. That manner, not without a trace of comic exaggeration, seemed to bring to life the expressive power of gestures contained in the poems. The humor in Kafka's own stories relies a great deal on such exaggeration and is often created through graphic descriptions of scenes that have the farcical character of theatrical comedy. It is a humor of gestures rather than of words, and it became especially apparent, as Brod says, when Kafka read from his own stories: "So zum Beispiel lachten wir Freunde ganz unbändig, als er uns das erste Kapitel des *Prozeß* zu Gehör brachte. Und er selbst lachte so sehr, daß er weilchenweise nicht weiterlesen konnte" (Brod 1962, 217). Brod does not deny the dark character of this laughter, but maintains that there was in it an "Einschlag von Welt- und Lebensfreude" (Brod 1962, 217). The humor in Kafka's description of Josef K.'s sudden arrest is indeed of a dark color. But what gives it that dark color is not so much the actual unfolding of the events as it is their sinister implications, implications that the reader seems more aware of than Josef K. to whom the arrest represents at this point primarily an irritating and unnecessary embarrassment. It is in the depiction of the figures carrying out and watching this arrest and in K.'s somewhat petty reactions that much of the story's humor lies.

K. is told by the "Aufseher" that he is lucky in the assignment of his guards, but these two men, Franz and Willem, do not distinguish themselves through their professional conduct. In some ways their behavior reminds one of the characters of *Alice in Wonderland*. First, they examine K.'s nightshirt, then they devour his breakfast and finally they offer to bring him, if he has money, another one from the diner across the street.   Then there is the old couple watching the entire episode from the house next door, moving with ruthless curiosity from window to window so as not to miss the events as they shift from K.'s bedroom to the landlady's living room and finally to Fräulein Bürstner's bedroom.   And there are the three employees from the bank where K. works in some elevated position (high enough for him to dine occasionally at the bank director's villa).   These three, Rabensteiner, Kullich and Kaminer, a German, a Czech and a Jew,[33] according to the "Aufseher" have been "provided" to make it easier for him to go to his office on this day without attracting attention with his late arrival. Like his two guards, these bank employees represent for K. contemptible subordinates, "niedrigste Organe" (R 263). They display a clownish eagerness to help him (all three run to get his hat), and one of them smiles continually because of a chronic muscle spasm, a smile "über das einen Spaß zu machen leider die Menschlichkeit verbot" (R 272).

The caricature-like features of Kafka's figures and the aspect of near-slapstick humor in their behavior stand in strange contrast to the dark and fateful background of the arrest.   K.'s attempt to take a quick swig in the secrecy of his bedroom ends abruptly when the "Supervisor" so startles him with the call to come back out that his teeth clatter against the brandy glass.   Late that evening K. waits for Fräulein Bürstner to apologize for using her room.   He finds himself caught in an awkward position when she finally arrives because he has forgotten to turn his light on.   He does not want to step out of his dark room, because that might look like an attack and frighten her, but he has to attract her attention quickly before she disappears into her own room, and so he is forced "in seiner Hilflosigkeit" to whisper her name through the crack of his slightly opened door.   Still later, when he reenacts for her the scene of his arrest that morning, he so forgets himself in the role of the shouting Supervisor that he wakes up the boarder in the next room, who protests by angrily banging against the wall. Such elements of caricature and farce are characteristic of Kafka's novels; they bring to mind the drawings of Wilhelm Busch which represent so well in a comic light the frailties of human nature and the pitfalls of life.

When K. in a final outburst of irritation at the relentless curiosity of his two aged neighbors shouts at them "weg von dort" (R 269) he reminds one of Papa Fittig in Busch's story "Plisch und Plum." Fittig's neighbor, Kaspar Schlich, has the unpleasant habit of coming by whenever there is trouble, only to utter the words: "Ist fatal. . . . Hehe! aber nicht für mich."[34] Fittig becomes more infuriated by each visit until he finally drops a big German pancake on Schlich's head, forcing him to admit that this time things are disastrous for him too. K.'s outburst is less effective but it results in a wonderfully comic pantomime acted out by the old couple and a third figure, a man with a reddish goatee, who has joined them: "Die drei wichen sofort ein paar Schritte zurück, die beiden Alten sogar noch hinter den Mann, der sie mit seinem breiten Körper deckte und, nach seinen Mundbewegungen zu schließen, irgendetwas auf die Entfernung hin Unverständliches sagte. Ganz aber verschwanden sie nicht, sondern schienen auf den Augenblick zu warten, in dem sie sich unbemerkt wieder dem Fenster nähern könnten" (R 268).

Like Busch's drawings, Kafka's scene represents a curious mixture of deep pessimism about human nature and a certain affection for the "human all-too-human." The unfeeling curiosity of the neighbors strikes us as funny because in their obsession not to lose a moment of the action next door, they remind us of children and of the fact that human beings tend to act like children all their lives. Similar to Busch's figures they are seen, one might say, from a great distance, "sub specie aeternitas," lending them a kind of metaphysical dimension.   This dimension becomes more "visible" in Kafka's stories than in Busch's (as in K.'s arrest by a mysterious agency), and in this sense, Kafka's figures are moving in a different sphere.   But his humor is characterized by a certain quality that reminds one very much of Busch's drawings, a quality that might be described as a distant yet affectionate vision of humanity.   It is this vision that makes bearable the dark dimensions implied by Busch's funny drawings and Kafka's comic descriptions, and the laughter that goes with this vision is, in the final analysis, not directed against human life but is on the side of human life.

III

Kafka's deep affection for human life manifested itself in many ways, such as in his love affair with the Yiddish theater, to be discussed in the next chapter, in his expressive manner of reading the Chinese poems or in the humorous aspects of his works.   It is important for our understanding of his relationship to language to remember that he did feel what Brod describes as "Welt- und Lebensfreude," for such feelings also influenced the character of this relationship.   He was capable of taking great pleasure in language, sometimes playing with it the way a child plays with a marvelous toy, at other times gripped by its power as though it were a steam engine (T 60).   He regarded with wonder the diversity of its manifestations, he was delighted by its aesthetic qualities and was moved to capture these qualities with further language. His love of language expressed itself also in the way he wrote *about* language.   His diaries and letters contain countless descriptions of words, sentences, speech mannerisms and conversations, so that one might well say that language itself represented one of Kafka's favorite subjects.   His characterizations of different languages and dialects show that his imagination reacted to them on a variety of levels, being struck by its concrete qualities, its sounds, its rhythms, as well as by its more intangible dimensions. Language represented the material he had to work with as an artist, and he regarded it always with an artist's eye and imagination, feeling out the words for their aesthetic and emotional potential. The German "Fürstin," for example, a word "ganz auf Pracht und Breite ausgerichtet," seemed to him without any of the "Liebe, Bewunderung und Zartheit" contained in its Czech equivalent "knežňa" (F 249).

He was also struck by the tangible characteristics of languages and dialects. Thus, he notes of the Berlin dialect: "das gehauchte Berlinerisch, in dem die Stimme Ruhepausen braucht, die von 'nich' gebildet werden" (T 70). He describes French as "kurzatmig mit seinen rasch aufeinander folgenden Ventilen" (T 159), and says of Czech that it occasionally affected his "German ear" like a fist blow (M 48 f.). The sound of a French word in a "sad German performance" (of one of Henri Meilhac's operettas) had a "good effect" (T 272), the American accent and idioms used by a "Jewish gold digger" who had recently returned from the U.S., made the man's German "restless" and allowed his "Jargon" (Yiddish) "to take a break" (T 621).

Sometimes Kafka conceived of sentences in terms of fanciful pictures, as he did in the following critique of one of his own stories: "Die ungeordneten Sätze dieser Geschichte mit Lücken, daß man beide Hände dazwischen stecken könnte; ein Satz klingt hoch, ein Satz klingt tief, wie es kommt; ein Satz reibt sich am andern wie die Zunge an einem hohlen oder falschen Zahn; ein Satz kommt mit einem so rohen Anfang anmarschiert, daß die ganze Geschichte in ein verdrießliches Staunen gerät . . . " (T 142). Sentences like broken fences, dissonant notes, hollow teeth, clumsy marchers, and a story that raises its eyebrows in irritation over all the clatter. Kafka may at times have complained about the difficulties he was having "with metaphors" (T 550), but as this passage shows, besides his problems with them, he also had an amazing command over metaphors, and he liked to use them especially when he talked about language.

At other times he described a bit of language purely for the sake of pleasure, as in a letter to Sophie Brod, Max Brod's sister, describing the title of a novel he had just seen someone reading on the train. The title *Der Tag der Vergeltung* suggests to him the picture of a flag: "Der 'Tag' ist eine Fahnenstange, das erste 'der' sind die Pflöcke unten, das zweite 'der' ist die Seilbefestigung oben, die 'Vergeltung' ist ein, wenn schon nicht schwarzes, so dunkles Fahnentuch, dessen Sichdurchbiegen vom 'e' zum 'u' durch einen mittelstarken Wind (besonders das 'ng' schwächt ihn) hervorgerufen wird" (Br 88).

Often he resorts to metaphoric descriptions to express his thoughts and feelings about his relationship to language. And as is characteristic for him he formulates these thoughts and feelings in pictures, in very physical, visual images: "Vor allem aber die Mitte alles Unglücks bleibt. Ich kann nicht schreiben. . . . Mein ganzer Körper warnt mich vor jedem Wort, jedes Wort, ehe es sich von mir niederschreiben läßt, schaut sich zuerst nach allen Seiten um; die Sätze zerbrechen mir förmlich, ich sehe ihr Inneres und muß dann aber rasch aufhören" (Br 85). Words, like obstinate little creatures, refuse to be formed into sentences, and sentences, when finally formed, fall apart again at once like poorly assembled wind-up toys whose emerging inner mechanisms destroy all semblance of life. The sight of these inner mechanisms puts a temporary end to Kafka's writing. The concept of mechanical construction plays an important role in Kafka's poetics (see especially Chapter Four), in that for him a good story had to have the qualities of a living organism and could show no traces of artificiality. His greatest problem with writing, perhaps, was the difficulty of creating literature he himself could consider alive in this sense. While the language that had to serve as his medium sometimes obeyed his commands even before he had conceived of them: "Wenn ich wahllos einen Satz hinschreibe . . . ist er schon vollkommen" (T 42), at other times, and it seems, more often, it would present him with sentences that fell apart like broken wind-up toys.

Always, he viewed language as a poet does, casting it in a variety of roles and finding striking pictures to describe it. His imagination responded especially to spoken language with childlike intensity. He visualized vowels "flying along like a ball" (T 9), words as "cold-eyed" nutcrackers (M 48 f.), sentences that moved like the wind. Thus in describing Dr. Rudolf Steiner's manner of delivering a lecture on theosophy, he writes: "Im allgemeinen fängt der gesprochene Satz mit seinem großen Anfangsbuchstaben beim Redner an, biegt sich in seinem Verlaufe, so weit er kann, zu den Zuhörern hinaus und kehrt mit dem Schlußpunkt zu dem Redner zurück. Wird aber der Punkt ausgelassen, dann weht der nicht mehr gehaltene Satz unmittelbar mit ganzem Atem den Zuhörer an" (T 52; cf. also T 129).

Again and again Kafka conceived of spoken language in concrete images. The empty "Kraftausdrücke," i.e., expressions like "furchtbar, riesig, ungeheuer, famos," come like "big rats" out of the "little mouths" of the Berlin girls (F 563 f.). The words of three "pious, plainly eastern Jews" singing the Kol Nidre (the song for the eve of Yom Kippur, the "Day of Atonement") seem to him spun out like molten glass: behind each one "werden Arabesken gezogen aus dem haardünn weitergesponnenen Wort" (T 72). At a poetry recital, the artist's voice "takes hold" of the words "so gently that they jump up" and have to be brought "back to earth" with "some sharp consonant or other" (T 265). And Kafka describes himself savoring Goethe's sentences "als liefe ich mit meinem ganzen Körper die Betonungen ab" (T 249).

Words, too, possessed for him tangible qualities: "Adieu" has such "Flugkraft" that it seems to carry away with it the words next to it (F 93). When Felice Bauer, Kafka's fiancée, talks of the "persönliche Note" their future furniture is to have, Kafka, who secretly dreads these domestic arrangements, notes in his diary that such an expression can only be pronounced "knarrend" (T 459).

In this way one might say that Kafka's view of language was dominated by his artistic inclinations and concerns. Yet in his daily life he also had to compose reports, official letters, speeches and similar documents for an insurance company. A panoramic picture of his relationship to language should include, besides his pleasure in language, the pain it caused him. Because he had a talent for writing, this work may have seemed an easy and convenient way for him to support himself, but in reality it tormented him. This emerges from the following entry in his diaries:

> Beim Diktieren . . . im Bureau. Im Schluß, der sich aufschwingen sollte, blieb ich stecken. . . . Endlich habe ich das Wort "brandmarken" und den dazu gehörigen Satz, halte alles aber noch im Mund mit einem Ekel und Schamgefühl, wie wenn es rohes Fleisch, aus mir geschnittenes Fleisch wäre (solche Mühe hat es mich gekostet). Endlich sage ich es, behalte aber den großen Schrecken, daß zu einer dichterischen Arbeit alles in mir bereit ist und eine solche Arbeit eine himmlische Auflösung und ein wirkliches Lebendigwerden für mich wäre, während ich hier im Bureau um eines so elenden Aktenstückes willen einen solchen Glückes fähigen Körper um ein Stück seines Fleisches berauben muß. (T 76 f.)

Kafka had great difficulties combining his writing with his work in the *Arbeiter-Unfall-Versicherungsgesellschaft* (to be discussed in Chapter Four). The time he had to devote to that work disrupted his writing (which he considered his true calling and sometimes referred to as his "work") (cf. e.g., Br 453), and frequently made it impossible to finish a story. Often he found himself completely incapable of writing during the brief intervals free from work. It was at such a moment of despair over the lack of "time for a story" that he sadly observed: "Ich lebe nur hier und da in einem kleinen Wort, in dessen Umlaut (oben 'stößt') ich zum Beispiel auf eine Augenblick meinen unnützen Kopf verliere. Erster und letzter Buchstabe sind Anfang und Ende meines fischartigen Gefühls" (T 59 f.). The word he is referring to occurs significantly in the description of how, if there is time, a story can be "experienced from its beginning," approaching like a steam engine before which the author runs along "aus eigenem Schwung" and at the same time driven by it "wohin sie nur stößt und wohin man sie lockt" (Br 60). All of Kafka's longing to express freely his creative drives is encapsulated in the word "stößt." The vowel of this single syllable, whose first and last consonants seem to begin and end a momentary release of energy (a *Stoßseufzer*), may remind him of the way fish seem to emit short sighs by opening and closing their mouths. Like them, he is condemned to remain mute.

Thus for Kafka a single word could embody his thoughts and emotions about writing, simply by virtue of the way it looked and sounded. One might say that this represented for him one of the great powers of language: its ability to express things on a level beyond the lexical dimension of words, on a level where words functioned more like gestures, communicating through their physical character: "Notwendigkeit, über Tänzerinnen mit Rufzeichen zu sprechen. Weil man so ihre Bewegung nachahmt, weil man im Rhythmus bleibt und das Denken dann im Genusse nicht stört, weil dann die Tätigkeit immer am Schluß des Satzes bleibt und besser weiterwirkt" (T 271). In this way the quality of one's sentences can communicate a great deal of nonverbal meaning. The rhythm of the dancers, the energy and excitement of their movements, the elation of watching them, can all be best expressed not through any particular words, but through the tone of one's voice, the emphasis with which one speaks. Thoughts are not allowed to come between the experience and its expression, and one's language, infused with the qualities of the experience, is capable of prolonging its effect. Kafka's remark about how to speak of dancers contains, in this sense, a condensed formulation of his poetics.

As will be discussed in the next chapter, languages, for Kafka, were inseparably connected with their cultural context. And just as a language can become much more intelligible when we see it surrounded by its living culture, words can be understood more fully through the gestures accompanying them, the circumstances under which they are spoken, the actions that go along with them, the special qualities of the speaker. The figures in Kafka's stories possess a rich repertoire of characteristic gestures. His diaries are filled with striking and very detailed descriptions simply of the way the people he encountered talked and moved. Mannerisms and gestures serve to characterize his figures as much as their words, and these words themselves derive a large part of their meaning from the demeanor and the behavior of the figures. Speech and gesture, from Kafka's perspective, were inseparable.

IV

The inseparability of speech and gesture applies to the figures in his stories as well as to the people he encountered in his daily life. What they said and how they said it fascinated him endlessly so that "Tatbeobachtung" constituted for him one of the most attractive and comforting aspects of his writing (cf. T 563). Above all he was struck by the role language played in the course of the interactions between the people around him, in their conversations, for he saw in these conversations the human bonds that tied them to each other and to the world, bonds from which he felt himself increasingly excluded. The ability to engage in conversations effortlessly came to stand for being firmly rooted in the human community and in a coherent world, for having one's feet safely on the ground. Thus he makes the following observation in his diary in January 1912:

> Der Umschwung, den ein Gespräch nimmt, wenn zuerst ausführlich von Sorgen der innersten Existenz gesprochen wird und hierauf, nicht gerade abbrechend, aber natürlich auch nicht sich daraus entwickelnd, zur Sprache kommt, wann und wo man einander zum nächsten Mal sehen wird und welche Umstände hierbei in Betracht gezogen werden müssen. Endet dieses Gespräch auch noch mit einem Händedruck, so geht man mit dem augenblicklichen Glauben an ein reines und festes Gefüge unseres Lebens und mit Achtung davor auseinander. (T 229)

The conversation seems to have a kind of rhythm of its own, like a dance, in that the participants follow its moves spontaneously and with natural ease. Communication occurs on several levels. Worries are shared, and the next meeting is agreed upon, but beyond that, without words, feelings of friendship and mutual support are expressed, and the final handshake generates a reassuring sense of harmony. That he perceived human conversation as the medium of such a sense of harmony is significant for our understanding of his attitude toward language. It shows that, rather than viewing language with fundamental skepticism and distrust, he saw it as a positive force capable of binding together human beings and anchoring them securely in the world. And it points to another way in which he himself can be said to have had a problem with language, for his growing inability to engage in the kind of conversation he describes in his diary became for him symbolic of his failure as a human being.

Kafka valued conversations immensely. He compares the effect of a peaceful face and quiet talk to hearing the voice of God from a human mouth (T 346). He notes down for himself rules for having a good conversation: "Man muß förmlich, um ein gutes Gespräch zu erreichen, die Hand tiefer, leichter, verschlafener unter den zu behandelnden Gegenstand schieben, dann hebt man ihn zum Erstaunen. Sonst knickt man sich die Finger ein und denkt an nichts als an die Schmerzen" (T 245). A few weeks later he describes a very different kind of conversation. His mother is chatting in the next room with the "Couple L." about house pests and corns. What they are saying has little significance, they might as well be talking about the weather, for the actual meaning of the words does not matter much. It is not the purpose of a conversation like this to communicate information or ideas: "Man sieht leicht ein, daß durch solch ein Gespräch kein eigentlicher Fortschritt eintritt. Es sind Mitteilungen, die von beiden wieder vergessen werden und die schon jetzt ohne Verantwortungsgefühl in Selbstvergessenheit vor sich gehn" (T 273). Overhearing conversations of this kind had a curious effect on Kafka. On the one hand, they had "empty spaces" that needed to be filled with reflections or daydreams in order to be made tolerable (T 273 f.). And there were times when all conversations, even the ones about literature, became intolerable: "Gespräche nehmen allem, was ich denke, die Wichtigkeit, den Ernst, die Wahrheit" (T 311). Sometimes he even felt that conversations contaminated him (Br 121), not because of their meaningless character, but rather because he felt him-self "seduced into self-observation" by his contact with people (H 98).

On the other hand, it is probably correct to say that Kafka would have given anything to be able to participate comfortably in the ordinary conversations of the people around him. For his inability to communicate easily with people became for him symbolic of his failure to prove himself a worthy member of the human community. He describes his unsuccessful life in a letter to Brod: "Ich habe in der Stadt, in der Familie, dem Beruf, der Gesellschaft, der Liebesbeziehung . . . der bestehenden oder zu erstrebenden Volksgemeinschaft, in dem allen habe ich mich nicht bewährt . . . " (Br 195). This failure, he felt, made him a social outsider who was best suited for observing the life of other people from afar: "Die für mich passendste Situation: Einem Gespräch zweier Leute zuhören, die eine Angelegenheit besprechen, die sie nahe angeht, während ich an ihr nur einen ganz fernen Anteil habe, der überdies vollständig selbstlos ist" (T 325). In Kafka's fragmentary "Beschreibung eines Kampfes" (1904-1905), a brief episode occurs that represents a good example of this kind of situation. One of its figures, the "Beter," in order to describe his dismal spiritual condition, tells about a childhood memory of overhearing a leisurely conversation between his mother and a woman in a garden. The episode is inserted into the narrative in the way a picture might be shown during a lecture to provide a vivid illustration of what is said. Such an illustration, without many words, can sometimes capture a complex point in an instant. The picture Kafka chose must have been charged with meaning for him in this way, for he first used it in one of his very early letters to Brod. The two had known each other for almost two years, but it was not easy for Kafka to develop an intimate relationship, and he used the garden conversation in his letter, it would seem, to communicate to his friend the things he could not say (Br 28 ff.).

This letter, a curious blend of personal communication and literature, talks about being overcome by the sudden impulse to look for "Klarheit über uns," and then lists a number of things that happened to its author during the summer. Its opening sentence, "Es ist sehr leicht, am Anfang des Sommers lustig zu sein," indicates that, as its last sentence says, summer is coming to an end. For the writer has been overcome by melancholy and can no longer go out dancing and falling in love with girls in white dresses. He has realized that, metaphorically speaking, he is being blown about by every current in the air, that he lacks the firmness with which other people are able to carry the burden of life. This realization is brought about by, among other things, a little conversation between his mother and a neighbor: "Als ich an einem andern Tag nach einem kurzen Nachmittagsschlaf die Augen öffnete, meines Lebens noch nicht ganz sicher, hörte ich meine Mutter in natürlichem Ton vom Balkon herunter fragen: 'Was machen Sie?' Eine Frau antwortete aus dem Garten: 'Ich jause im Grünen.' Da staunte ich über die Festigkeit, mit der die Menschen das Leben zu tragen wissen" (Br 29).

As already mentioned, the episode appears in only slightly altered form in the "Beschreibung eines Kampfes." There the "Beter" precedes his account of the conversation with the request to let him know "wie es sich mit den Dingen eigentlich verhält, die um mich wie ein Schneefall versinken" (B 91). These are the "worries of innermost existence" that Kafka was trying to become clear about and express in his letter to Brod. The "schwankende Unglück" (B 85) of the "Beter," his "Seekrankheit auf festem Land" (B 89), makes him invent the most "random" names for the things in the world, such as "tower of Babel" or "Noah when he was drunk" for "the poplars in the field," because he is no longer satisfied with their "wahrhaftige" name (B 89). He reminds one in this respect a little of the young writers of the "Prague

Circle" whose lack of firm artistic ground drove them to use an artificial and elaborate language. But clearly, he represents primarily an aspect of Kafka himself, i.e., his sense of spiritual and artistic lack of roots, his vision of the world and the human relationships around him disintegrating as in falling snow, his feeling that his literary language had lost the "true name of things."

In contrast, the conversation between his mother and the neighbor is, in a wider human sense, still using the "true name of things," for it evolves naturally and effortlessly between human beings securely anchored in their world: "Sie sagten es ohne Nachdenken und nicht besonders deutlich, als hätte jene Frau die Frage, meine Mutter die Antwort erwartet" (B 91). The dancelike ease of the conversation, its spontaneity and natural progression reflect an existential stability that the "Beter" has lost. He is, one might say, no longer at home in this world and its language has slipped away from him so that, as a person, he can only observe it from the outside, as an artist, can only "pour" random names on it.

It is important to keep in mind that the "Beschreibung eines Kampfes" was written in 1904-1905, that is, a time when Kafka was still preoccupied with overcoming the "Schwulst" of the "Prague Circle" and finding a pure and natural language for himself. This preoccupation, however, had even then a dimension beyond questions of literary aesthetics, i.e., a dimension concerning "the firmness with which people are able to carry life" and the task of living the good life. Kafka's ideal of participating in the good life by founding a family, of living "dans le vrai" (Brod 1962, 96, 122), must have begun to haunt him as he was approaching thirty and becoming more and more aware of his own inability to realize that ideal. For in the entries of his diary from 1910 till August 1912, that is, *before* he met Felice Bauer, he returns to the subject of marriage again and again

(T 150, 160, 173, 198, 199, 216).

The dismal fate of the bachelor is the theme of a lengthy undated entry from the year 1910 that reads like a companion piece to the "Beschreibung eines Kampfes." While that story begins at a party inside a house, the passage from the diary takes place in front of a house where a party is in progress. In both texts, a conversation occurs between the narrator of the story and a character who stands in such close relationship to the narrator that the two seem like different aspects of the same person. The narrator in the diary is eager to participate in the party, his partner, a bachelor who identifies himself as the narrator's guard, tries to convince him that he really does not want to go. Both of them quickly turn to the subject of being unmarried.

The conversation seems like an overture to Kafka's work from 1912 on in that it contains many of its themes and motifs. The guard complains that it makes no difference whether he joins the party or not, because the people there won't pay attention to him crawling along under his construction of "ceremonies" like an "Ungeziefer"(T 18). The narrator who wants to join the party even if he has to get up the stairs "by somersaulting," falls into a long description of the life of the bachelor. Such a man suddenly becomes aware of his fate, like someone who suddenly notices a "Geschwür" on his body and can from that moment on only focus on it. At the end of his monologue the narrator is no longer talking about "the bachelor," but rather about "us." "Till now," he says, "our nose was sticking in the stream of time, now we step back, former swimmers . . . and are lost. We are outside the law, nobody knows it, yet everyone treats us accordingly" (T 22). In these passages from Kafka's diary, there are some of the central themes and leitmotifs of his "Die Verwandlung," *Der Prozeß*, "Ein Landarzt," "Der Jäger Gracchus" and "Die Sorgen des Hausvaters," as well as a foreshadowing of the writer's own unsuccessful efforts to return within "the law," his ill-fated "Heiratsversuche" (H208). Symbolic of his being "outside the law" became the fact that he could not talk to people. There are numerous remarks about this inability of his in his diaries and letters. One of them, often quoted to document his skepticism toward language, comes from a letter to his friend Oskar Pollak:

> Wenn wir miteinander reden: die Worte sind hart, man geht über sie wie über schlechtes Pflaster. Die feinsten Dinge bekommen plumpe Füße und wir können nicht dafür. . . . Wenn wir miteinander reden, sind wir behindert durch Dinge, die wir sagen wollen und nicht so sagen können, sondern so herausbringen, daß wir einander mißverstehen, gar überhören, gar auslachen. . . . Wenn wir es zu schreiben versuchten, würden wir leichter sein, als wenn wir miteinander reden, — wir könnten ganz ohne Scham . . . reden. . . . (Br 9 f.; cf.also T 202, 359, 385, 403, 406, 411, 460, 468, 473, 514, 565, 580; Br 119, 163, 286; F 85, 401, 402, 422, 448, 452)

In his "Brief an den Vater" he accuses his father of having deprived him of his ability to speak. Any quiet conversation with the father, an overbearing man, tyrannically critical of his children, was impossible. According to Kafka his father's angry "Kein Wort der Widerrede!" so stifled him as a boy, that he "unlearned to talk" and began to speak in a "hesitating, stuttering manner" (H 175). This, Kafka says, affected his entire life.

Brod, discussing the letter in his biography of Kafka, assumes that Kafka was referring with this remark only to his encounters with his father, for in social situations, Brod says, when Kafka actually did talk, which happened rarely, he spoke "durchaus frei, leicht, elegant und mit gewinnendem, überströmendem Einfallsreichtum, der sehr oft scherzhafter

Art und immer verblüffend natürlich, alles andere als 'stok-
kend' war" (Brod 1962, 33).   Other reports of personal encounters with Kafka emphasize, like that of Brod, that he
was extremely shy and quiet.[35] Kafka described himself as
"menschenscheu und ängstlich" (H 195).   His relationship to
other people, he felt, was permanently encumbered by his
childhood memories of the way his father would abuse the
employees working in his wholesale "Galanteriewaren" business.[36]   In his adult life Kafka was able to overcome his
instinctive reluctance to enter relationships with people only
to a limited extent.   When he did, as with Felice Bauer or
Milena Jesenská, he expressed himself primarily through
letters.   As he grew older, he suffered more and more
acutely from his inability to simply chat with people. "Wie
kann andere Menschen als mich das Plaudern freuen!" he
writes in his diary in 1922 (T 571).

In 1923, a year before his death, in a letter to Brod,
explaining why he hasn't written for a long time, he confes-
ses that he had "strategic reasons," for he no longer trusts
words and letters, especially letters (Br 452; cf. also M 259).
When he was twenty years old, he thought that letters might
be an easier way for him and his friend Pollak to communicate; now, two decades later, he no longer sees even this
possibility. Kafka's most serious problem with language, we
might say, consisted in his inability to relate to others in
conversation. Cut off from most people by this inability, he
poured himself into countless letters but never felt that this
was a satisfying substitute for direct human contact. In the
end it seemed that only art could offer what Kafka cherished
the most: " . . . manchmal scheint mir das Wesen der Kunst
. . . die Ermöglichung eines wahren Wortes von Mensch zu
Mensch" (Br 453).

In the following chapters I will draw a picture of the
problems that arose for Kafka in writing literature.   As
already suggested by the figure of his "Beter," the loss of

human contact had given Kafka a sense of isolation not only from people but also from their world. In terms of literature he felt at an early point in his life that he was letting slip away the "true name of things," that his language, just as he himself, had no firm footing in the world. Yet almost a decade later he wrote "Das Urteil," a work that in all likelihood represented even for him the "true name of things." His struggles to achieve such a level of truth in art, and his complex relationship to his own cultural roots and the language of his literature will be the subjects of the rest of this study.

2

Jargon
Kafka's Search For Roots

Kafka liked to think of his stories as growing "organisms" that, if "entitled" to a place in the existing "organization of the world," would carry within themselves their own structure, similar perhaps to the seed that carries within itself the potential for a complete plant (T 450). The picture of the work of art as a living form whose right to existence within a culture depends in some sense on its own inner organization is very characteristic of Kafka's self-understanding as a writer. He despised literary "constructions," creations, as Brod says, "ohne den Atem organischen und immer unerwartet hervorblühenden Lebens" (cf. T 331, 339, 375, 435, 463; Br 70, 95 f., 159, 192, 213 f.; Brod 1962, 33 f.).

In despair over one of his stories Kafka once asked: "Wie will ich eine schwingende Geschichte aus Bruchstücken zusammenlöten?" (T 498). The contrast between the "organism" of a "vibrant story," in which the parts fall into place naturally, and the forced "construction" of a text in which the parts are assembled according to some artificial scheme, plays a central role in his poetics. For Kafka judges literature according to standards of "purity" and "truth" (T 534), "harmony" (T 75), "order" (T 34, 105, 116, 142) and the "real" (T 379); and he condemns it in terms of "wrong" and "fragmented" (T 161 f.), "merely schematic" (T 375) and "mechanical" (T 435). Good work is connected "word by word" with the writer's life (T 39), bad work seems "too far from the heart" (T 377).

That Kafka thought of his writing in this way cannot be ignored when one seeks to understand his conception of language. For his tendency to think of the world as an organization of organisms, a place of *natural* order where individual life-forms evolve through growth and development, will importantly affect his view of language. This view does not exist in isolation but rather belongs in a certain context of ideas and culture. That context has its immediate roots in the German literature of the eighteenth century, particularly in the writings of Johann Gottfried Herder. To Herder it was important to look at language not as a dead system of signs, but rather as a spontaneous expression of the human spirit, a complex organism that develops according to the laws of nature from childhood to old age.[37] A similar perspective was taken by the philologists Jakob and Wilhelm Grimm and Wilhelm von Humboldt.[38] In the twentieth century, Karl Kraus became the greatest, the most vocal representative of this understanding of language as a life form.

Although Kafka never expressed the kind of language mysticism one finds in the writings of Karl Kraus,[39] he applies artistic standards to language that show a distinct affinity to the Viennese writer. These standards demand of the work of art "organic" character, i.e., that it be grown in accordance with internal natural laws, and that it be true and pure in this sense. Kraus, like Kafka, contrasts organisms with constructions. "Der Satz," he says, "ist eine Gestalt und nicht bloß Konstruktion" (KW II 103). In the work of a good writer form and content represent the same kind of unity as body and soul, in the works of bad writers, they only are as body and dress (KW III 111). Words must become the "naturnotwendige Verkörperung" of thoughts. The "Geheimnis organischen Wachstums" (KW III 114) consists in the fact "daß die Sprache den Gedanken nicht bekleidet, sondern in ihn hineinwächst" (KW III 325 f.). The concept of organism is applied by Kraus to words (KW II 289) as well as language (KW II 436). Language, he says, is ruled by "Naturgesetzlichkeit" (KW II 436) so that true works of literature represent "organisches Leben" (KW II 220) or, just as for Kafka, organisms and not constructs (KW III 245).

Hand in hand with his emphasis on the natural, not constructed nature of language goes Kraus' denial that language is "Verabredung" (KW II 245), a deliberately established system of signs. Instead language emerged as the result of spontaneous human reactions to the world. Color words, for example, are like little poems in that they represent instinctive responses of the human mind to striking visual experiences: "Jedes Wort ist ursprünglich ein Gedicht und was den Vollbegriff des Dings umfaßt, ist ihm nur abgelallt. Wäre es anders und wäre die Sprache wirklich das, wofür die Menschen sie halten, ein Mittel, sich nicht mit der Schöpfung, sondern über sie und über sie hinweg zu verständigen . . . wäre es gleich besser, sich   jener Konventionen, jener akustischen Stenogramme zu bedienen, die auf einem Kongreß beschlossen werden . . . " (KW II 381).[40]   Unlike Kraus, Kafka did not theorize a great deal about the nature of language.   In his diaries and letters are only a few passages in which he deals with language on an abstract level (F 305, 341).   The majority of his observations concern the actual language used by actual people, be they the servants of his parents or his literary friends in Prague.   Yet it can be argued plausibly that the spirit of his conception of language comes very close to that of Kraus in that he too regarded words as organically connected with people's lives, an expression of their whole being, that could perhaps give them complete access to the "Herrlichkeiten des Lebens": "Es ist sehr gut denkbar, daß die Herrlichkeit des Lebens um jeden und immer in ihrer ganzen Fülle bereitliegt, aber verhängt, in der Tiefe, unsichtbar, sehr weit. Aber sie liegt dort, nicht feindselig, nicht widerwillig, nicht taub. Ruft man sie mit dem richtigen Wort, beim richtigen Namen, dann kommt sie. Das ist das Wesen der Zauberei, die nicht schafft, sondern ruft" (T 544). For both Kraus and Kafka it is characteristic to think of language not merely as a rational and convenient communication device but rather as a basic feature of human existence, deeply rooted in the souls of human beings, inseparably connected with their lives and possessing powers that far transcend its purely descriptive function.

Such an understanding of language entails necessarily the view that there is a fundamental connection between people's lives and their language and that the whole character of a language is determined by the life-style of its speakers. That Kafka looked at language in this way emerges from his lecture on "Jargon," which he gave in 1912 as an introduction to a recital of Yiddish poetry by the Polish actor Jizchak Löwy, a favorite of Kafka's.[41] In this brief lecture about the Yiddish language Kafka draws a colorful picture of that peculiar linguistic phenomenon, and he does so mainly by describing the character of the people who use "Jargon," the hurried life-style from which it grew.

As Brod reports, Kafka organized the evening of the recital almost single-handedly, taking care himself even of the "technical arrangements," thus showing how much "un-released energy and activity slept inside of him" (Brod 1962, 139). Kafka tries in his talk to reassure his audience who, as he knows, is largely unfamiliar with the Yiddish language.[42] This audience, it may safely be assumed, consists primarily of well-educated middle-class Jewish members with an interest in literature and Jewish culture. Some of these members may have had grandparents who still spoke Yiddish, certainly most of them have ancestors who used the language in their daily lives. Kafka is aware that presenting this audience with a Yiddish poetry reading is likely to produce a negative emotional response, a response he describes as "Angst mit einem gewissen Widerwillen." For, as he had just read a month before in Pinès' *Histoire de la littérature judéo-allemande* (Paris, 1911) (T 242), there had been all through the nineteenth century a conscious effort on the part of educated European Jews to rid themselves and ultimately all their people of what they considered the stigma of the Yiddish language.[43]

This language, the language of Ashkenazic Jewry, i.e., of the Jewry that settled in central and eastern Europe, was spoken in the nineteenth century in most countries with a Jewish population.[44] Documents in this language date back as far as the fourteenth century so that one may assume that it began to develop earlier. Its linguistic origins are Hebrew (and Aramaic) which the Jewish settlers brought with them from their homeland, and Old and Middle High German, the language of the areas these settlers had moved into.[45]

By 1500 and still at Kafka's time Yiddish was spoken throughout eastern Europe, where over the years it had absorbed a great deal of Slavic and had developed, as Kafka mentions in his lecture, into numerous regional dialects. What is called by linguists "western Yiddish,"[46] the Yiddish spoken in western Europe, had virtually disappeared, having been extinguished by the cultural assimilation efforts of western European Jewry, the despised Haskole. "Eastern Yiddish," however, continued to be spoken and was carried by Jewish emigrants to other parts of the world. (Today "Yiddish" always refers to eastern Yiddish.) Kafka saw both, the established middle class circles of Prague's small population of German-speaking Jewry (about 10% of the total population) (cf. Wagenbach 1958, 71)[47] and the large groups of Yiddish-speaking emigrants moving through the city on their way to some new homeland. As was customary in Prague then,[48] he called the first "Westjuden," the second "Ostjuden."

These two categories were to become of key importance in Kafka's understanding of himself and his place in the world as the "most western Jewish of the western Jews" (M 247), an importance that began to crystallize during his encounter with Löwy's theater company. Kafka's initial interest in the "Jargon" theater—he had been introduced to it by Brod (Brod 1962, 137 f.)—reflected a certain trend of the late nineteenth and early twentieth century, a new concern with the neglected Yiddish language and a new appreciation of its special status among the other European languages. Such new concern and appreciation expressed itself in the movement to standardize the Yiddish language and raise it to a literary level.[49] And in an increase in the production of literature for entertainment, which had been sparse up to then.[50]

Pinès' *Histoire* must be considered written in this spirit of regeneration. The author takes a strongly disapproving attitude toward the assimilation movement, which by radically suppressing the Yiddish language had effectively extinguished the Yiddish culture of "western" Jewry. There are parallels between Pinès' emotional, at times polemical, attacks on the Jewish Enlightenment (Haskole) and the rebellion in romantic literature against a rationalism that failed to recognize the power of folk songs and folktales.[51] Yiddish was the natural medium for folkloristic and popular Jewish literature, and out of this medium, Pinès and others like him hoped, a mature literature would develop.[52] One might consider the movement to rehabilitate the Yiddish language as a kind of romantic movement, the expression of a new awareness of the importance of one's cultural roots.[53]

The development of the Yiddish theater, which began in the late 1870s,[54] was closely linked to this movement, and Kafka's sudden passion for the actors from Lemberg (Lvov) and their performances (as well as his subsequent and lifelong love for the "eastern Jews") has a distinctly romantic flavor. The energetic organizational efforts Kafka made on behalf of the actors reflect an inspired optimism he did not often feel. In his diary he notes in connection with his contribution to that evening: " . . .   stolzes, überirdisches Bewußtsein während meines Vortrags . . . starke Stimme, müheloses Gedächtnis. . . . Da zeigen sich Kräfte, denen ich mich gern anvertrauen möchte, wenn sie bleiben wollten" (T 251). Looking back at this time two years later, he wistfully writes to Löwy: "Es kommt mir vor, als wären wir beide viel hoffnungsvoller gewesen, als wir an den Abenden in Prag herumzogen" (Br 129).

However, it was not just Kafka's enthusiasm for the Yiddish theater that had a romantic flavor, but, more importantly, the spirit of his lecture itself, in which he attempts to persuade an unsympathetic and possibly embarrassed audience to open their hearts and minds to a poetry that will put them in touch with their lost cultural roots.   He merely hints at these roots by suggesting that there might be special powers in his audience enabling them to understand the unfamiliar Yiddish.   A review from the Jewish weekly *Selbstwehr* of a Yiddish song recital during the same time in Prague formulates the thought quite explicitly:

> The purpose of the folksong evening was to allow our Prague Jewry to gain an enjoyable insight into the popular psychology of the Eastern Jews; and to this purpose was joined the hope that among our allegedly completely assimilated Western Jews kindred chords would stir, (that) their own Jewish feeling, usually buried by the impressions of their environment, would

respond to a sympathetic element, and that from the Eastern Jewish poetry, there would also grow a permanent strengthening and revival of our own inner Judaism.[55]

Kafka's involvement with the Yiddish theater must be understood in the context of this general movement for cultural Jewish self-awareness and regeneration. To reassure themselves of a positive cultural identity the "western Jews" had to become reacquainted with their forgotten roots. That was the message behind his evening of Yiddish poetry. For the Jewish families who, like his, strove to assimilate to the German culture in order to secure a more respectable and therefore safer social status, Yiddish represented a painful reminder of the ostracisms and persecutions suffered by their people.

Because of its raggedy and makeshift character, Yiddish had no respectability, so that Heinrich Graetz, in his widely read *Volkstümliche Geschichte der Juden,*[56] contemptuously calls it "lallendes Kauderwelsch."[57] Kafka had read this book, like Pinès', "gierig und glücklich" as he says in his diary (T 132), during the first few weeks of his involvement with the Yiddish theater company, to provide, one might say, a kind of accompanying commentary on that experience. The work that Kafka owned was a three-volume version of Graetz's great eleven-volume history of the Jewish people, *Geschichte der Juden von den ältesten Zeiten bis auf die Gegenwart* (1853-1876), and it, like the book by Pinès, provided him with a context within which the phenomenon of the Yiddish language could be understood.[58]

This language had no standardized grammar to speak of.[59] It existed in a state of permanent change because the unstable living conditions its speakers so often were faced with forced it to adapt to new environments and situations continuously. It represented a motley assembly of linguistic bits and pieces and seemed an unlikely candidate for a literary medium.[60] Yet Kafka had fallen in love with it[61] and was now asking his probably less favorably disposed audience to try to let go of their anxieties and prejudices regarding Yiddish and allow themselves to relate freely to the language, which was, after all, part of their past.

They have, he assures them, resources inside of themselves that will enable them to understand the unfamiliar language: "Ganz nahe kommen Sie schon an den Jargon, wenn Sie bedenken, daß in Ihnen außer Kenntnissen auch noch Kräfte tätig sind und Anknüpfungen von Kräften, welche Sie befähigen, Jargon fühlend zu verstehen" (H 426). For this reason he advises them not to be preoccupied with the fact that they can't understand the words but rather to focus on their sounds and rhythms, the quality of the recital and the actor himself. For this actor comes from Poland and in many ways represents the traditional Yiddish culture lost to the "western" Jews in the audience. As emerges from letters to Felice Bauer, Kafka found Löwy tremendously attractive because of his vivacious temperament and flamboyant gestures. He refers to him as "'ein heißer Jude,' wie man im Osten sagt" (F 77), a man whose passionate spirits cannot be repressed and who is therefore irresistibly appealing to the author (F 392, 396).

Kafka notes down in his diary a description of Löwy reciting poetry that captures vividly the intensely emotional style of this actor. With gestures bordering on the melodramatic, Löwy makes a direct and personal appeal to his audience:

Löwy verkrampft beim Rezitieren die Haut der Stirn und der Nasenwurzel, wie man nur Hände verkrampfen zu können glaubt. Bei den ergreifenden Stellen, die er einem nahebringen will, nähert er sich uns selbst oder, besser, er vergrößert sich, indem er

seinen Anblick klarer macht. Nur ein wenig tritt er
vor, hält die Augen aufgerissen, zupft mit der ab-
wesenden linken Hand am Schlußrock und hält die
rechte offen und groß uns hin. Auch sollen wir, wenn
wir schon nicht ergriffen sind, seine Ergriffenheit
anerkennen und ihm die Möglichkeit des beschrie-
benen Unglücks erklären. (T 241 f.)

Accompanying one's speech with lively gestures is considered characteristic of many nations in the world, but for
European Jewry, aspiring to assimilate to the culture of their
respective countries, these gestures became, just like their
Yiddish dialects, a humiliating stigma.[62] The conscious efforts of several generations to suppress such ethnic mannerisms—there were books published on this subject[63]—had no
doubt left their mark on Löwy's listeners, and his dramatic
gestures were bound to make them uneasy. But for Kafka
these gestures belong to the Yiddish language, express its
very essence. That is why he urges the audience to focus
on *them* in order to understand the words. By submerging
themselves in Löwy's performance they will be able to enter
the poetry in spite of its unfamiliar language, for "Jargon ist
alles, Wort, chassidische Melodie und das Wesen dieses ostjüdischen Schauspielers selbst" (H 426).

Kafka's brief but intense involvement with the Yiddish
theater company directed by Löwy in the winter of 1911-
1912 was primarily the expression of an increasing awareness
of and need for his own Jewish heritage (cf. Brod 1962,
137). From the following entry in his diary it emerges that
it was more the actors (especially Löwy) than the plays they
performed that satisfied this need: "Die Eindrucksfähigkeit
für das Jüdische in diesen Stücken verläßt mich, weil sie zu
gleichförmig sind. . . . Bei den ersten Stücken konnte ich
denken, an ein Judentum geraten zu sein, in dem die Anfänge
des meinigen ruhen und die sich zu mir hin entwickeln und

dadurch in meinem schwerfälligen Judentum mich aufklären und weiterbringen werden, statt dessen entfernen sie sich, je mehr ich höre, von mir weg. Die Menschen bleiben natürlich und an die halte ich mich" (T 234).

As his mistranslation of the title of the Yiddish play "Di Shkhite" (The Slaughter) as "der, welcher Schächterkunst lernt" shows, Kafka initially understood almost no Yiddish (T 173; cf. Wagenbach 1958, 179),[64] but must have become proficient quickly. He exposed himself to the language by attending numerous performances and spending long nights with the actors themselves. A comment from his diary shows how attentively he observed the speech habits of his new friends. He remarks on a certain speaker's custom of interspersing his sentences with frequent phrases like "Ladies and Gentlemen," "honored guests," etc. He adds: "So weit ich aber Löwy kenne, glaube ich, daß solche ständige Wendungen, die auch im gewöhnlichen ostjüdischen Gespräch oft vorkommen, wie "Weh ist mir!" oder "S' ist nischt" oder "S' ist viel zu reden" nicht Verlegenheit verdecken sollen, sondern als immer neue Quellen den für das ostjüdische Temperament immer noch zu schwer daliegende Strom der Rede umquirlen sollen" (T 243). Three years later, he is still impressed by the vitality and forcefulness of the "eastern Jewish" speech mannerisms which made those of the culturally assimilated Prague Jewry seem feeble and inadequate by contrast: "Max, das Ungenügende, Schwächliche seiner Rede . . . . Dagegen ein gewisser W., zugeknöpft in ein elendes Röckchen . . . schmettert Ja und Nein, Ja und Nein" (T 465).

In addition to steeping himself in spoken Yiddish through contact with the Polish theater company, he read that winter, as already mentioned, Pinès' history of Yiddish literature. In his diary he remarks on how deeply he enjoyed the book, reading it "gierig, wie ich es mit solcher Gründlichkeit, Eile und Freude bei ähnlichen Büchern noch niemals getan habe"

(T 242). Here, he learned about the origins and the development of this strangely heterogeneous language; the implications of its history for "Westjuden" in general and for himself in particular must have struck him powerfully. These implications could only reinforce his sense of cultural rootlessness and personal isolation, for by renouncing Yiddish educated European Jewry had deprived itself of one of its very basic traditions. Whatever language took its place could not offer the emotional and spiritual attachment that would have bound its speakers naturally to Yiddish. Abandoning it must have seemed to Kafka the equivalent of cutting off one of one's cultural taproots. For besides numerous loan words, Yiddish also contained many important words from Hebrew, thus providing its speakers with a direct link to their ancient cultural origins.[65]   Kafka's intense involvement with the Yiddish theater, whose performances, after all, bordered according to Brod on the "Unfreiwillig-Komische" and "Kitsch" (Brod 1962, 138), is easier to understand if one takes into account that to Kafka the Yiddish plays, providing a warm and living context, offered access to his lost roots.

It is remarkable and says a great deal about Kafka's general sense of language how quickly he developed an understanding and feeling for Yiddish. At the beginning of October 1911 he saw Löwy's company for the first time, presumably barely able to follow the lines of the play (cf. Wagenbach 1958, 116). A few months later, toward the end of the following February, he introduces Löwy's poetry reading with a strikingly insightful talk about the character and linguistic peculiarities of this "mißachtete" language (H 423). He describes Yiddish as a restless language in continuous flux, consisting almost exclusively of a perpetual stream of loan words which enter the language and disappear again like popular migrations: "Völkerwanderungen durchlaufen den Jargon von einem Ende bis zum anderen" (H 422). It is a mobile language whose words by their "Neugier und Leicht-sinn" constantly threaten to upset its status quo, so that great strength is required to hold it together (H 423). Because of its special relation to German, Yiddish cannot be translated into this language: "'Toit' zum Beispiel ist eben nicht 'tot' und 'Blüt' ist keinesfalls 'Blut'" (H 425).

Kafka does not develop here for his audience the unfortunate consequences this fact may have for German-speaking Jewry, but a few weeks earlier, he touches on these consequences in his diary. He realizes, he says there, that he has never been able to love his mother as much as she deserved, because the German language prevented it. " . . . wir geben einer jüdischen Frau den Namen deutsche Mutter, vergessen aber den Widerspruch, der desto schwerer sich ins Gefühl einsenkt. 'Mutter' ist für den Juden besonders deutsch, es enthält unbewußt neben dem christlichen Glanz auch christliche Kälte, die mit Mutter benannte jüdische Frau wird daher nicht nur komisch, sondern auch fremd" (T115f.). The German word "Vater," too, is wrong and "meint bei weitem den jüdischen Vater nicht" (T 116). The problem here is not only that the traditional language of family life has been lost but also that there is no adequate replacement. Because German, which is adopted as the socially proper and culturally desirable language, introduces an element of rigidity, correctness and implied standards (to be socially acceptable, one must speak German), it can never become a comfortable language for family life. Even years later, Kafka tells Milena Jesenská that, while German is natural for him since it is his mother's tongue (his mother came from a wealthy German-speaking family) (cf. Wagenbach 1958, 20 f.), Czech has for him a much warmer quality, "ist mir viel herzlicher" (M 22). German remains for him a cold language.

In the context of his family, the influence of the German standards is so pervasive that even behind the more congenial word "Mama" Kafka feels compelled to imagine the word "Mutter." To Kafka "Mutter" and "Vater" seem to have disturbing and incongruous overtones, but since they are the only words at his disposal (the only words encouraged at home, for Kafka spoke Czech, his father's language, fluently, and was taught French as a child by the obligatory governess) (cf. Wagenbach 1958, 26),[66] he really has no names for his parents with which he can relate to them in a warm and easy-going way. That his relationship to his parents was not warm and easygoing certainly had a variety of reasons, many of which he himself discusses in his famous "Brief an den Vater." It was not only the somewhat artificially imposed German that caused the tensions in the Kafka household, but the fact that this language was spoken at all appeared to Kafka symptomatic of what lay at the root of his family's conflicts. Jewish families like his, he felt, had lost all cohesion by renouncing their cultural traditions, or, as with respect to religion, by merely continuing these traditions in a meaningless, "sanitized" form.[67] Nothing in their present lives held these families together, so that, as Kafka says in his diary, "nur noch Erinnerungen an das Ghetto die jüdische Familie erhalten" (T 116).

Once, after observing a group of "eastern Jews," he notes wistfully in his diary: " . . . das selbstverständliche jüdische Leben. Meine Verwirrung" (T 486). Clearly he felt excluded from the existence of these people who still led lives anchored securely in the traditions of their religion and language. Some years later he describes a large group of Russian-Jewish emigrants awaiting their American visas in the Jewish courthouse in Prague. Here too he expresses a sad yearning to belong among these people, and he wishes he could be one of the little boys running around among the grown-ups, without worries, their families nearby (M 220 f.). His painful sense of homelessness, the awareness of his own spiritual and emotional alienation from what he considers his roots, affects his work in many ways, its themes and concerns as well as its style.

Emblematic of this state of homelessness is the German language, his all-important artistic medium, yet not the language of his heart. Kafka's deep intellectual and emotional reservations about his relationship to German language and literature will be discussed in the next chapter. These reservations represent the other side of his attraction to the traditions of east European Jewry. The strong sense of cultural identity he found there was precisely what he missed so completely when he wrote his dazzling German sentences. In this respect Kafka can be said to have had a serious problem with language; but his love for the Yiddish language and all that belongs with it does not seem problematic in the same way.

For besides the negative feelings of cultural loss he associated with that language, he had a very positive appreciation for Yiddish as an intriguing and colorful linguistic phenomenon with a vital place and function in the lives of particularly mobile human beings. The perspective he took here tells us a great deal about the way Kafka looked at language generally. It shows that philosophical skepticism did not play an important part in his considerations. Throughout his diaries and letters, almost all of his observations about language are of a concrete nature and concern specific aspects of actual language rather than abstract philosophical issues. When he became interested in "Jargon," he was struck by a number of linguistic features of the language and even more by the way it expressed so accurately the spirit of the people who spoke it, their impatient temperament and mobility reflected perfectly in its very words. Both these aspects of Yiddish he touched upon in his brief lecture about "Jargon."

This lecture reflects his familiarity with the history of the German language and linguistic concepts such as the one he uses to explain certain differences between Yiddish and German, for example, the concept of "Wahlform," which refers to the development of different forms that the same word may assume in separate regional dialects (H 423). As Max Brod told Klaus Wagenbach, Kafka was very interested "an allem Sprachlichen" and frequently discussed with him philological questions such as the "Bedeutungswandel von Wörtern, die ins Deutsche entlehnt wurden" (Wagenbach 1958, 116). But Kafka's interest in language went beyond such theoretical linguistic considerations. "Jargon," as his lecture shows, represented for him a fascinating phenomenon, in many ways like a living being. Most importantly it was intimately connected with the people who spoke it and the conditions of their lives. Its many loan words have assumed the "Eile und Lebhaftigkeit" of the way they were taken up by its speakers, and the "Gaunersprache" likes to borrow from it because this kind of language needs words rather than grammar (H 423).

In the case of "Jargon," in fact, the connection between the culture of the people and their language appears to Kafka so close that, as he somewhat playfully implies, the language can be understood simply by appreciating the spirit of its culture. Even those who no longer speak it may have access to it by focusing on its nonverbal aspects. This kind of understanding is different from guessing the meaning of words from their context, although that may come in sometimes. The "feeling" understanding of the Yiddish poetry that Kafka suggests is possible for his audience, goes beyond the lexical meaning of the words, involves a sense for the history and the character of a people and an appreciation of the aesthetic and moral qualities of their culture.

What Kafka is hinting at in his talk about "Jargon" is that a language can really only be understood in the context of the lives of the people who speak it. Without the customs and the life-style of a culture, without the circumstances surrounding it, the conditions its members must daily respond to, without all this, learning and understanding a language is very hard and probably impossible. This shows itself, for example, in the fact that in dictionaries of ancient languages such as Greek the authors often are unable to give simply an equivalent word for the Greek but have to resort instead to listing examples of uses of the word in the context of sentences. What color was Homer describing when he called the sea wine-dark or the dawn rose-fingered? The ancient Greek culture is in certain ways (not in all, fortunately) inaccessible to us; similarly inaccessible, although to a much lesser degree, was the culture of old European Yiddish-speaking Jewry to Kafka's audience. Assimilated Jewry had forsaken and forgotten the customs that went along with that language, the day-to-day life of which it was a part. Because families like Kafka's deliberately disassociated themselves from this culture, it had for all purposes disappeared from their lives.

But unlike the culture of ancient Greece, this culture could be revived, if only for an evening, through the Polish actor Löwy who came to the German-speaking and thoroughly assimilated Jewry of Prague like a messenger from a different world to let the language of that world, Yiddish, come alive. Kafka's involvement with the Yiddish theater was admittedly brief, but his intense interest and love for the "eastern Jews," nonassimilated east European Jewry remained a lifelong, everpresent feature of his imagination, as shown by such works as "Die Sorge des Hausvaters" (1917) or "Josefine, die Sängerin oder Das Volk der Mäuse" (1924). In these stories, written years after his encounter with the Yiddish theater, he embodied the mobility and the vivacity as well as the haunted character of the east European Yiddish-speaking culture.

Odradek, the object of the family man's cares, has been compared by Brod, and rightly so, to the image of the wandering Jew (Brod 1922, 60).[68] There are, however, positive aspects to this image for Kafka, for the little wooden creature is not only a restless spook but also colorful (if a little shabby) and attractive in its mobility, rather like a child's toy,[69] and the mouse folk, though leading a harassed and dangerous existence, have a certain splendor about them, simply by virtue of their vivacity and energy for living. Significantly Kafka's description of the children of the mice echoes a grimly proud passage from Graetz' *Geschichte*:

> Graetz: Für geweckte Knaben gab es keine Jugend, denn sie wurden früh genug von dem eisigen Hauch rauhen Lebens durchfröstelt und geschüttelt, aber eben dadurch wurden sie zeitig zum Denken geweckt und zum Kampf mit der lieblosen Wirklichkeit gestählt.[70]

> Kafka: In unserem Volk kennt man keine Jugend, kaum eine winzige Kindheit. . . . Unser Leben ist eben derart, daß ein Kind, sobald es nur ein wenig läuft und die Umwelt ein wenig unterscheiden kann, ebenso für sich sorgen muß wie ein Erwachsener. . . unsere Feinde sind zu viele, die uns überall bereiteten Gefahren zu unberechenbar—wir können die Kinder vom Existenzkampf nicht fernhalten, täten wir es, es wäre ihr vorzeitiges Ende. (E 194)

Kafka wrote this story shortly before his death, when he was already quite ill, and he may have written it in part to raise money for his hospital care, for he asked Brod to get it published for him as soon as it was finished. (The fact that Brod was successful within ten days may indicate something about Kafka's literary status at that time.)[71] It is remarkable what a powerful role the motif of eastern European Judaism plays in this last story. This may be partly a reflection of Kafka's love for Dora Dymant, the young woman who shared with him the last two years of his life, who came from a shtetl in Poland (cf. Brod 162, 239 f.), and who represented, as Löwy did many years ago, the eastern Jewish culture. However, the echo from Graetz' *Geschichte* points back into the past, to the days of the Café Savoy, when Kafka first became intoxicated with the fire of "hot" eastern European Judaism.

The beginning of "Die Sorgen des Hausvaters" similarly evokes the context of those days, for the mock philological report on the meaning (or lack of meaning) of the word "Odradek" reminds at once of the introductory chapter of Pinès' *Histoire*, which discusses the Yiddish language. German and Slavic, the two possible influences manifest in the word "Odradek," are also the two major European sources of Yiddish.   The story perfectly illustrates Kafka's attitude toward language.   Semantic studies are fine and good, but must yield to the facts of life.   The unsuccessful attempts to trace the history of the word "Odradek" and thus discover its lexical meaning seem pointless in the face of the paradoxical creature's actual existence.   If it did not exist, the family man asks, would anyone bother with such studies? (E 144).   And with this remark, he turns to Odradek, whose image must tell the reader what the semantic studies would not show.

Such preference for the concrete over the abstract was according to Brod characteristic of Kafka.   For when he began to come to terms with Judaism, he did not, like many of his friends, take the theoretical route of Zionism but chose instead the living experience of the colorful Yiddish theater (Brod 1962, 137 f.).   With his predilection for "Tatbeobachtung," the observation of individual people and their behavior, as opposed to the development of generalizing theories, Kafka was unlikely to give his work the kind of uniform philosophical underpinning of skepticism Susanne Kessler claims to find there.[72]   As his lecture on "Jargon" shows, language interested him as a living phenomenon, as well as an aspect of his personal artistic development.

In the context of Kafka's involvement with the Polish theater company there crystallized for him the problem of establishing a link to his missing cultural heritage.   This heritage must have seemed lost to him forever, embodied as he found it by a shabby group of wandering actors and the despised language of their plays. Given his family background and his strong dislike for anything artificial or forced, Kafka could never become a Yiddish writer,[73] yet he felt sadly that his "Hochdeutsch" cut him off from expressing warmth and intimacy. German was indeed, as Weltsch says, Kafka's "linguistic home,"[74] but during the winter 1911-1912 he felt much more at home with the Yiddish spoken by "the Jews at the Café Savoy" (T 93, 111).

3

The Stolen Child
Kafka's Sense of the
Illegitimacy of German-Jewish Literature

Klaus Wagenbach in his marvelously rich and sensitive biography of the young Kafka raises the question of how accurately the Prague author assessed his situation as a German-Jewish writer. The critic feels that Kafka had a tendency to overgeneralize his problems and to talk of "Germans" when he should talk of the Germans in Prague: "Manches, was hier als Eigenart und Situation des jüdischen Schriftstellers deutscher Sprache charakterisiert wird, ist von Prag aus gesehen" (cf. Wagenbach 1958, 91 f.).

Wagenbach is referring to a letter Kafka wrote to his friend Max Brod in 1921, a letter which will be discussed in detail toward the end of this chapter, for it contains indeed the "bedeutendste Äußerung Kafkas zur Sprache" (Wagenbach 1958, 92). In it, Kafka describes the literature produced by German-Jewish writers as a "Zigeunerliteratur, die das deutsche Kind aus der Wiege gestohlen und in großer Eile irgendwie zugerichtet hatte, weil doch irgendjemand auf dem Seil tanzen muß" (Br 338). Kafka's relationship to German literature is certainly closely connected with his relationship to its language, and both will be examined shortly. However, instead of restricting the perspective of the examination to the immediate situation in Prague at the turn of this century, its focus will be given a much wider range. For unlike Wagenbach, I feel that Kafka's problematic relationship to his writing was not the result of conditions limited to that particular place and time, but rather the outcome of historical and cultural developments beginning in the eighteenth century and affecting the entire assimilated European Jewry who had chosen German as the new language. (This is not to say that there were no German-Jewish writers who felt comfortable with their situation.) Kafka would have accordingly included Heinrich Heine in his "Gipsy literature," for he considered him as the epitome of the (German-Jewish) writer whose whole being is a lie (Br 397; cf. also Brod, Prager Kreis 40). And he does include Karl Kraus (who lived in Vienna)—not just as one of the Gipsies, but as their supreme master.

For Kafka, the problematic situation of the German-Jewish writer existed on a much larger scale than the city life of Prague. By the time he wrote the letter quoted by Wagenbach, through reading books like Pinès' *Histoire* and Graetz' *Geschichte*, he had grown familiar with the larger dimensions of the history of his "Gipsy literature." This history had become the framework of his self-understanding as a writer for it enabled him to make sense out of his feelings about language and literature. To appreciate fully Kafka's ambivalent attitude toward the medium of his art, the German language, one must be able to see this attitude in its larger historical and cultural context. It will therefore be necessary to include a great deal of the kind of material usually inserted into critical studies under the heading of "excursus." Since such a method of organization tends to obscure the intimate connections between the primary subject of the study (in this case Kafka) and the secondary material (here certain literary and cultural developments in the history of European Jewry), I do not wish to separate the two sharply. Instead I will draw a picture of Kafka *within* the framework of those developments, interweaving discussions of him with discussions of them as seems required by that picture.

Because it is only within such a framework that his attitudes toward writing and language can emerge clearly, only within their historical and cultural context that his artistic problems can become truly intelligible. As his diaries and letters show again and again, he is well-informed and acutely aware of the history of European Jewry and all his life sees and understands himself in terms of this context. Even when he is only nineteen years old and shows little knowledge yet of the Jewish traditions he is later to be so powerfully drawn to (cf. Wagenbach 1958, 41), he recognizes a certain problem he and his friend Oskar Pollak must face as a feature of their specific Jewish cultural background. He writes: "Weißt Du aber, was das Allerheiligste ist, das wir überhaupt von Goethe haben können, als Andenken . . . die Fußspuren seiner einsamen Gänge durch das Land . . . die wären es. Und nun kommt ein Witz . . . bei dem der liebe Herrgott bitterlich weint und die Hölle ganz höllische Lachkrämpfe bekommt—das Allerheiligste eines Fremden können wir niemals haben, nur das eigene—das ist ein Witz, ein ganz vortrefflicher" (Br 12). Kafka's language here is still marked by the influence of the *Kunstwart*, a Berlin journal devoted to poetry, theater and music, whose peculiar and rather artificial style tends to color Kafka's own at this time (cf. Wagenbach 1958, 102 ff.).[75] Yet the theme of the passage is one that will occupy him all his life: the apparent illegitimacy of German-Jewish literature. From a psychological point of view Kafka found the German language cold (M 22), from an aesthetic point of view "dried out" (T 26), and from a spiritual point of view it created a continuous crisis for Jewish writers like him, who, although, to all intents and purposes native speakers, could never feel truly at home with the German language, yet were driven by historical and cultural conditions to aspire to excel in it.

For speaking flawless German became in many cases part of the assimilation efforts of European Jewry and was from the outset closely connected to these efforts. Because one of the three fathers and founders of the Jewish cultural assimilation movement was Lessing's friend Moses Mendelssohn, for whom learning German meant not only learning a language, but also absorbing a literary culture about to reach its spectacular climax in the "Weimarer Klassik."[76] The attainment of this culture was from the outset a powerful motive behind the assimilation movement in central Europe. Mendelssohn's German, polished to perfection with the help of one of its great masters, Lessing,[77] is flawless and of remarkable lucidity. When his first book, the *Philosophische Gespräche* (1755), appeared, the reviewer in the *Göttingsche Gelehrten Anzeigen* believed it was Lessing who had published it anonymously.[78] In 1763, he won the first prize of the Prussian Academy in a philosophical writing contest, not, as Waxman says, because of the profoundness of his thought, but rather because of the clarity and order of his arguments.[79] (Kant received the second prize.)

Besides an improved social status, greater stability and prosperity, the attainment of the language of classical German culture, and that meant primarily the language of its literature, became one of the great priorities of the assimilation movement in central Europe. As Alexander Altmann says, Mendelssohn's German translation of the Pentateuch was specifically intended as a tool for teaching his sons Hebrew (which was printed side by side with the German), thus opening up for them the sacred text. But beyond this immediate purpose he envisaged a far reaching program for the intellectual and spiritual regeneration of his people in which the new German Bible translation was to be the "first step toward culture."[80]   At the time of the publication of Mendelssohn's Torah translation (1780-1783) only the educated upper-class Jewry spoke German.[81]   Thus, not many of the people whom this translation was to serve knew its language well enough to benefit from it, but the work, as Altmann points out, was really "addressed to the needs of the rising generation rather than of the old one."[82]   (One person belonging to this rising generation was, for example, the mother of Heinrich Heine. She was ten years old in 1780 and still used Hebrew characters and a "somewhat faulty" German in the letters of her youth.)[83]

Mendelssohn continued to urge that all Jewish people learn German. Thus, in 1782 he warns against the introduction of Yiddish or Hebrew into official legal language, which had been suggested in order to accommodate those who had not learned German yet. For he believes that dropping Yiddish altogether and adopting German wholeheartedly, as he had done, would be of great cultural and moral benefit to his people: "Hingegen würde ich es ungern sehen, wenn . . . die jüdischdeutsche Mundart, und die Vermischung des Hebräischen mit dem Deutschen, durch die Gesetze autorisiert werden müßte. Ich fürchte, dieser Jargon hat nicht wenig zur Unsittlichkeit des gemeinen Mannes beygetragen, und verspreche mir sehr gute Wirkung von dem unter meinen Brüdern seit einiger Zeit aufkommenden Gebrauch der reinen deutschen Mundart."[84]

Mendelssohn proposed German as the new standard language for his people primarily for the purpose of upgrading its spiritual life, the rejuvenation of the Jewish faith. But there were also other benefits, for at the end of the eighteenth century the German language had through the great wealth of its literature reached a true climax in its cultural development.[85]   And in the end it was more for the sake of the ideals of classical German culture than for the sake of Judaic faith (as envisioned by Mendelssohn) that Yiddish had to be dropped, the Jewish mannerisms and life-style suppressed, or as Felix Weltsch puts it, the Jewish historical consciousness be mutilated.[86]

Lessing's call for religious tolerance in the form of an early comedy *Die Juden*, and his famous later drama *Nathan der Weise*, whose central character is said to portray Mendelssohn,[87] may well have provided the assimilation movement with inspiration and moral support, for in these plays he represents Jewish characters who prove themselves through their actions to be ethical and wise.[88] Kafka must have been struck by the irony of fate that allowed the enlightened efforts of the great German writer to help bring about conditions that in the end would lead to the most painful cultural alienation of a generation of German-Jewish intellectuals who, after all, were still following the path that Lessing had helped Moses Mendelssohn to take.[89]

Heinrich Heine's family had followed this path.[90] The poet himself represents the greatest success among the German-Jewish writers, for he gave the Germans their most popular book of poetry (*Buch der Lieder*), which has become for them a standard wedding gift, and a national folk song ("Die Loreley"), which they look upon as one of their most distinctive trademarks. But Heine, unlike his assimilated family, maintained a problematic love-hate relationship to Judaism all his life,[91] and his contributions to German literature and middle-class tradition, his light-footed, elegant mastery of German prose, did not keep him from feeling somehow artistically disadvantaged and therefore inadequate, especially when he compared himself with the great champion, Goethe:

> In der Tat, Wolfgang Goethe hatte, um seine Gedanken auszusprechen, das ganze Arsenal der redenden Künste zu seiner Verfügung, er gebot über alle Truhen des deutschen Sprachschatzes, der so reich ist

an ausgeprägten Denkworten des Tiefsinns und uralten Naturlauten der Gemütswelt, Zaubersprüche,
die im Leben längst verhallt, gleichsam als Echo in
den Reimen des Goetheschen Gedichtes widerklingen
und des Lesers Phantasie so wunderbar aufregen! Wie
kümmerlich dagegen sind die Mittel, womit ich Ärm-
ster ausgerüstet bin, um das, was ich denke und
fühle, zur äußern Erscheinung zu bringen! (HSW VI
495)

In spite of its mocking over- and undertones, this
passage is profoundly serious and touches on the same
problem as Kafka does when he speaks of the "Allerheiligste
eines Fremden," i.e., Goethe's literary heritage, that can
never belong to people like him. The quote comes from
Heine's *Der Doktor Faust* (1851), a work in itself indicative
of Heine's predicament in that it is hopelessly competing with
the "großen mystischen Nationaltragödie Goethes" (HSW III
52) by putting up against it a strangely hybrid literary
creation consisting partly of a ballet libretto and partly of a
rather long scholarly essay about the "genesis of the Faust
fable" (HSW VI 478).[92]

Heine, one might say, represents the first sign of the kind
of cultural alienation so acutely felt by Kafka and his generation. This sense of estrangement expresses itself to a large
extent in Heine's uneasiness with traditional literary categories and concepts, his ironic undermining of such concepts,
his search for alternative forms.[93] But when he regretfully
admits that the "uralten Naturlaute der Gemütswelt" that were
available to Goethe no longer stand at his disposal, Heine is
not only rejecting the imitation of the old, but he is also
mourning its loss. For where Goethe commanded "all the
chests of the German language treasure," Heine finds himself
sadly reduced to "meager resources."

Karl Kraus, who came to despise Heine for what he

considered his facile lyrics and feuilletonistic prose,[94] would have agreed wholeheartedly with him here, for he says of him in his famous essay "Heine und die Folgen" (1910): "Das Geheimnis der Geburt des alten Wortes war ihm fremd" (KW VIII 213). For Kraus there could not have been a more profound criticism of a writer than to deny his ability to find access to the old ("das alte Wort") by spontaneously creating it anew, by, so to speak, giving birth to it once again.

The writer's problem of combining true originality with faithful adherence to existing standards of language occupied Kraus a great deal. These standards had been established for him, quite in keeping with the assimilative ideals first set down by Mendelssohn, by the language of classical German literature, and he had become their most militant defender in the twentieth century. In countless reviews, critiques and essays primarily published in his own journal *Die Fackel* he preached the gospel of classical High German, the epitome of which was represented for him, as for Heine, by the shining ideal of Goethe.[95]

To solve the problem of preserving the German language in its most highly developed classical state while creating through it something altogether new and alive Kraus invented a kind of mythology of language: "Der Gedanke ist in der Welt, aber man hat ihn nicht. Er ist durch das Prisma stofflichen Erlebens in Sprachelemente zerstreut: der Künstler schließt sie zum Gedanken. Der Gedanke ist ein Gefundenes, ein Wiedergefundenes. Und wer ihn sucht, ist ein ehrlicher Finder, ihm gehört er, auch wenn ihn vor ihm schon ein anderer gefunden hätte" (KW III 236 f.). Language for Kraus represents a mysterious and awe-inspiring spiritual force existing quite independently of individual human minds; it enables poets and thinkers to fetch "preformed" thoughts "als Fertiges vom Himmel herunter" (KW VIII 205). "Kunst ist das Geheimnis der Geburt des alten Wortes," but a mere imitator—like Heine—is only "informiert und weiß darum nicht, daß es ein Geheimnis gibt" (KW III 292).

Kraus has two basic objections against Heine. First, and most disastrously, it was in Kraus' opinion this poet who gave rise to the "Utilliteratur" and "Impressionsjournalistik" of the modern press, i.e., a style of writing that describes "keinen Beinbruch . . . ohne Stimmung," a slick and facile use of manipulative language that dresses up banal news stories in pretentious emotionality (KW VIII 193). But obviously Kraus is not simply condemning Heine for something the poet can hardly be held responsible for, the influence he exercised on journalists long after his death. The second and much more severe charge made by Kraus against Heine is therefore that he writes "Operettenlyrik" (KW VIII 201), poetry that cynically dresses up ready-made moods (KW VIII 200) for the audience and is designed primarily to appeal to middle-class German sentimentality. And so to Kraus Heine's words seem not the "naturnotwendiger Ausdruck" of genuinely felt experiences but merely ornament, "skandierte Journalistik" (KW VIII 202).

In contrast, the poetry of Detlev von Liliencron (1844-1909) represents "tiefere Stimmungen" and is therefore placed side by side with Goethe's (KW VIII 200). Liliencron wrote nature poetry in a spontaneous, simple, yet intensely lyrical language and was stereotyped by his contemporaries as uncomplicated, naive and in direct contact with his feelings.[96] Critics labeled him an "Originalgenie"[97] and a "Lyriker der germanischen Unmittelbarkeit."[98] Liliencron's close relationship to the landscape of his native Schleswig-Holstein, his ties to that landscape both through birth (he belonged to an old aristocratic, if poor, family from the area) and through inclination (he spent much of his time outdoors, hunting, horseback riding, always alive to his nature impressions)[99] made some of his contemporaries think of him as a somewhat simpleminded "Naturbursche." But for Kraus,

Liliencron's limited focus on the landscape of his birth had "cosmic" dimensions (KW VIII 208), and the poet's fresh, natural style, in which others found an affinity to the literature of folklore, was seen by Kraus as the "wilde Jagd Liliencronscher Sprache" (KW VIII 199). Kraus' words, by the way, were sure to arouse in every German reader reminiscences of Theodor Körner's poem "Lützow's wilde verwegene Jagd" which was set to music by Carl Maria von Weber and well-known throughout Germany. The poem describes the daring military feats of the famous Prussian major general Adolf Freiherr von Lützow during the Napoleonic Wars of 1813-1815, feats in which Körner participated and perished.

Neither Kraus' complete condemnation of Heine nor his somewhat extravagant praise of Liliencron should be considered objective and definitive judgments.[100] Seen in the larger framework of Kraus' efforts to stem the "intellektuellen Schmutzfluten" in Germany (KW VIII 208), to prevent the "Verwüstung am Worte Goethes" (KW II 56), in short, to preserve the standards of classical German literature, Heine und Liliencron became like allegorical figures representing the good and the bad: Liliencron firmly rooted in Schleswig-Holstein and the German language, Heine drifting about in the world (he spent much of his life in exile in Paris) with only a superficial relationship to his medium. His lack of roots (KW VIII 208) rendered him incapable of writing genuine poetry, for such poetry can only be written "als Offenbarung des im Anschauen der Natur versunkenen Dichters" (KW VIII 208).[101]

Ironically, Liliencron considered himself as Heine's "geringsten Schüler,"[102] but then the north German poet did not see the world divided into the rightful inheritors of the classical spirit of Weimar and literary impostors, con men who were only flaunting stolen goods. For it would never have occurred to Liliencron to question the legitimacy of his own or anyone else's use of the German language and he might well be said to represent one of those speakers whose German, as Kafka says, is truly alive. In a letter to Brod in 1921, Kafka formulates in bitter words what lies at the heart of Kraus' hatred for Heine and love for Liliencron. Kraus has realized, he writes, " . . . daß im Deutschen nur die Dialekte und außer ihnen nur das allerpersönlichste Hochdeutsch wirklich lebt, während das übrige, der sprachliche Mittelstand, nichts als Asche ist, die zu einem Scheinleben nur dadurch gebracht werden kann, daß überlebendige Judenhände sie durchwühlen." (Br 337)

Liliencron does not belong in the "kleine Welt der deutsch-jüdischen Literatur" Kafka is describing here (Br 336), but to the diametrically opposite world of cultural roots and legitimacy where the "most personal High German" is alive, that is, where German has been spoken as the traditional language of the family for generations. Liliencron is a perfect representative of this kind of German speaker, all the more as he also has strong ties to the landscape he grew up in, and much of his poetry consists in spontaneous expressions of his responses to nature. Thus, for Kraus, he approaches the ideal of "Erlebnislyrik" associated especially with Goethe and Weimar classicism.[103]

There are no comments about Liliencron's work in Kafka's diaries, although it is almost certain that, already as subscriber to the *Kunstwart*, where some of Liliencron's poems were published (cf. Wagenbach 1958, 103), and definitely as an avid Kraus reader,[104] he was familiar with it and also had heard the north German read from his work in Prague in 1902 (cf. Wagenbach 1958 103, 126, 221).[105] But regardless of Kafka's views of the quality of his poetry, one may safely assume that for him Liliencron represented a German poet by birthright whose language was truly alive and who for better or for worse had a legitimate claim to participation in the literature of his country.

Two writers who also are in Kafka's sense truly at home
with the German language, and whom he does mention, are
Theodor Storm (1817-1888) and Eduard Mörike (1804-1875).
He describes an encounter that took place between the two in
a letter to Brod from the year 1922. Storm had recorded the
experience of a visit to Mörike in a short memoir. The great
delight with which Kafka read this memoir is reflected in his
affectionate retelling of the story: "Diese beiden guten
Deutschen sitzen im Frieden dort beisammen in Stuttgart,
unterhalten sich über deutsche Literatur, Mörike liest 'Mozart
auf der Reise nach Prag' vor (Hartlaub, Mörikes Freund, der
die Novelle schon sehr gut kennt, 'folgt der Vorlesung mit
einer verehrenden Begeisterung, die er augenscheinlich kaum
zurückzuhalten vermochte. Als eine Pause eintrat, rief er mir
zu: 'Aber i bitt Sie, ist das nun zum Aushalte'.— Es ist
1855, es sind schon alternde Männer, Hartlaub ist Pfarrer)
. . . " (Br 397).

A feature of this literary encounter that is hard to convey
in a translation but that must have seemed extremely significant to Kafka, is that both Mörike and Hartlaub were letting
a great deal of Swabian dialect slip into their sentences. This
fact surprised Storm, for it was not customary in north
Germany to mix Low German with High German in one's
conversations (SSW VIII 30). When reading his novella,
however, Mörike according to Storm dropped "jeden Anflug
von Dialekt" (SSW VIII 30). Quite naturally, he considered
the informal character of what Kafka calls in a different
context the "vertrauliche Verkehrssprache" (H 425) as
inappropriate for his literary work. Thus Mörike used the
relaxed regional dialect the way one might slip into and out
of a comfortable pair of house shoes. In a similarly easygoing spirit, Storm's father, who comes to pick up his son,
bursts out into Low German when Mörike suggests that he is
Swiss: "Ach wat . . . ick bün man en Westermöhlner
Burjung!" (SSW VIII 35). Although Kafka read Storm's

little memoir a year after formulating his view that German only lives in dialects and the "most personal High German," this memoir seems a perfect illustration of that view. Both Storm and Mörike speak and write a highly developed literary language which nevertheless exists within, and firmly tied to, a context of regional dialects, and has, in this sense, living roots.

The conversation also turns to Heine, whose *Buch der Lieder* Storm considers along with Goethe's *Faust* as one of the two "Zauberbücher" that opened for him the door to German literature (SSW VIII 19). Mörike treasures among his "handschriftliche Raritäten" a Heine poem with many corrections by its author (SSW VIII 34). He considers Heine a "Dichter ganz und gar" but adds: "nit eine Viertelstund' könnt' ich mit ihm leben, wegen der Lüge seines ganzen Wesens" (SSW VIII 29). This remark, Kafka says, represents a summary of his own view of the writer (in general—not just of Heine), and he concludes with characteristic irony: "Den Talmudkommentar dazu her!" for he has touched on a subject of truly spiritual dimensions (Br 397).

Heine did have a reputation for being insincere, of saying one thing and meaning another, if the circumstances made it convenient.[106] For example, he apparently never told his wife Mathilde that he was Jewish, as emerges from an anecdote in Alfred Meißner's *Geschichte meines Lebens* (1884).[107] Kafka read this book, as Brod reports, during his stay in the health resort Schelesen in 1918 (Brod, Prager Kreis 28) and two years later relates the anecdote in a letter to Milena (cf. also Br 247). Thus he was aware of Heine's dishonest character, but this negative feature of Heine's personality can hardly have been what made him generally representative of "the Writer" for Kafka. Mörike's comment about Heine has a distinctly personal character. It is like saying "I love New York but I wouldn't want to live there." He admires Heine's poetry greatly, but dislikes him as a person. Kafka, however, for whom perhaps person and writer are not as easily separated, takes the comment as expressing a fundamental truth about Heine, the writer, as well, a truth he declares as universally applicable, but that probably relates mainly to himself and the other German-Jewish writers of his generation.

It is easy to see why Storm's account made a deep impression on Kafka, for in it, as in a kind of morality play, he found a representation of the two major aspects of his literary existence: the distant world of German literature, idyllic in its cohesiveness, and his self-destructive efforts to become part of it, efforts which, like Heine's, were doomed from the outset because of the "lie of his whole being." This literature, Kafka thought, lay far beyond the "small German-Jewish world" (Br 336) of writers like Kraus and Kafka, and remained "jedem jüdischen Zugriff unzugänglich" (Br 400). Even if such a writer were to get up day after day at four in the morning and plough the area around Nürnberg from one end to the other for his entire life, Kafka says sarcastically in another letter to Brod, the landscape would not "answer" him (Br 400). But, one might add, the landscape of Schleswig-Holstein will answer Storm or Liliencron at a moment's notice.

In the "small German-Jewish world," which once had begun so brilliantly with the inspired friendship of Lessing and Mendelssohn,[108] now according to Kafka an entire generation of young Jewish intellectuals found themselves in the "schreckliche Lage" of trapped insects: "Weg vom Judentum . . . wollten die meisten, die deutsch zu schreiben anfingen, sie wollten es, aber mit den Hinterbeinen klebten sie noch am Judentum des Vaters und mit den Vorderbeinchen fanden sie keinen neuen Boden" (Br 337). The problem of his generation, Kafka feels, crystallizes in the young Jewish writer's relationship to his language and he therefore calls it a "problem of language," yet adds that it might also be called

something entirely different (Br 338). He does not elaborate
this point, but the implications of his words seem to be that
it would be wrong to think of his generation's plight as
concerning language alone. Rather, this plight involves the
entire being of the young German-Jewish writers, their
outlook on life and culture, their place in that culture, their
sense of identity based on that place, their relationship to
each other and many more aspects of their situation.

Their problem is, Kafka says, the impossibility of writing
German literature, or any other literature, combined with the
impossibility of not writing (Br 338). And this problem has
become especially visible in the figure of Kraus, whom he
declares the absolute master of the art of "Mauscheln" (Br
336). This verb according to Grimm's *Deutsches Wörterbuch*
means to talk and act like a "schacherjude". Heine, for
example, uses it in this sense when he describes the Polish
Jews (HSW VII 194), but Kafka gives it a new definition.
For him it is the "laute oder stillschweigende oder auch
selbstquälerische Anmaßung eines fremden Besitzes, den man
nicht erworben, sondern durch einen (verhältnismäßig)
flüchtigen Griff gestohlen hat und der fremder Besitz bleibt,
auch wenn nicht der einzigste Sprachfehler nachgewiesen
werden könnte. . . . Ich sage damit nichts gegen das
Mauscheln, das Mauscheln an sich ist sogar schön, es ist eine
organische Verbindung von Papierdeutsch und Gebärden-
sprache . . . " (Br 336). In the "Gipsy literature" of the
"small German-Jewish world," Kafka says, "Mauscheln"
provides just about the only possible form of expression (Br
336). It represents the rope dance of the German child stolen
from its cradle (Br 338).

Kafka touches here on a subject that (as his remark about
Goethe's "Allerheiligstes" quoted at the beginning of this
chapter shows) occupied him all his life. The problems of
the German-Jewish writers, their sense of illegitimacy, their
lack of close emotional bonds to their language, their feelings

of cultural isolation, are reflected in the recurring theme of human alienation in his fictional writing. The unsuccessful attempts of the outsider to become an insider is the theme of his three unfinished novels: The sixteen-year-old Karl Roßmann, sent to America by his parents because he impregnated a servant girl, must establish himself in the bewildering world of his new homeland; Joseph K., propelled out of his successful middle-class existence by the arrest through a mysterious legal system, strives in vain to gain entrance to the laws of this system; the stranger K., looking like a vagabond but claiming to be the land surveyor, arrives in "the village" to seek both acceptance into its community and employment by "the castle" to which the village belongs. Outsiders also appear in many of Kafka's shorter pieces of fiction, e.g., Gregor Samsa, isolated from his family by the terrible appearance his body has assumed; the tamed ape who has assimilated with human society and writes a report "for the academy" about his experiences; the haunted figure of the Hunter Gracchus who cannot die and must (like his little cousin Odradek) forever roam up and down the steps of the "big staircase leading upwards" (E 272).[109]

In a letter to Milena, Kafka says of his friend Max Brod: "Er . . . hat keine Heimat und kann deshalb auch auf nichts verzichten und muß immerfort daran denken, sie zu suchen oder zu bauen . . . " (M 173).[110] Of himself, Kafka draws a still darker picture: not a peaceful second is given to him, nothing is given to him, he must acquire everything, even the past (M 247). As Brod records, Kafka once calls himself and Brod "nihilistic thoughts rising in God's head," but he explains to his worried friend that these thoughts are only the result of a bad divine mood: God had a bad day. Brod asks: "So gäbe es außerhalb unserer Welt Hoffnung?" Kafka's reply: "Viel Hoffnung—für Gott—unendlich viel Hoffnung—, nur nicht für uns" (Brod 1962, 95).

Any interpretation of Kafka's work has to take into

account the powerful role the picture of the outsider played in his imagination. While his sense of alienation from the world has much affinity with certain universal feelings of modern man, it should not be forgotten that this sense grew directly out of the cultural and spiritual alienation experienced by some members of assimilated European Jewry. That this phenomenon would have particularly profound implications for the Jewish artist is to be expected and shown by Kafka's case. The serious problems this writer was experiencing with language involved no abstract linguistic or philosophical concepts, but rather the actual sentences he spoke and wrote, and the problem arose from certain cultural and spiritual features of his historical situation.

This situation was, as Kafka remarks, for his generation of German-Jewish writers still dominated by Goethe and his language: "Goethe hält durch die Macht seiner Werke die Entwicklung der deutschen Sprache wahrscheinlich zurück. Wenn sich auch die Prosa in der Zwischenzeit öfters von ihm entfernt, so ist sie doch schließlich, wie gerade gegenwärtig, mit verstärkter Sehnsucht zu ihm zurückgekehrt und hat sich selbst alte, bei Goethe vorfindliche, sonst aber nicht mit ihm zusammenhängende Wendungen angeeignet, um sich an dem vervollständigten Anblick ihrer grenzenlosen Abhängigkeit zu erfreuen" (T 212). Kafka's language, which does not resort to "obsolete idioms" (except in the letters from his *Kunstwart* days), nevertheless is marked by the standards of Weimar classicism, simply because he went to a humanistic *Gymnasium* where those standards were drilled into the students rather mercilessly. (As Wagenbach reports, an extraordinary amount of memorization was required from the students, Wagenbach 1958, 24). Besides the ideals of Greek and Roman antiquity, the model of classical German literature was held up to the students. The standards of the prose style taught, emphasizing the clarity and precision of classical German,[111] were probably more influenced by Schiller than

Goethe and shaped the German spoken by the educated
middle class including the state officials throughout Germany
and the Austro-Hungarian empire.[112] No wonder then that
Kafka's language should, in some ways, resemble that of the
k. k. *Kanzleisprache*, as is sometimes remarked.[113]

The German language had thus been standardized on an
amazingly wide scale, just as Goethe had been claiming in his
essay "Deutsche Sprache" (1818).[114] With it, one gained
access to that cherished "humanistisch-humanitäre Bildung"[115]
even if one lived in the provinces of the Austro-Hungarian
Empire. Thus, two of the greatest masters of the German
language in the twentieth century, Kafka and Celan, came
from those provinces (Celan from Bukovina, an area in the
northeastern Carpathian Mountains).[116] Many of the German
speakers in these regions were in fact Jewish. Their com-
munities and their schools represented as it were the outposts
of Weimar classicism in eastern Europe.[117] And it was the
schools that carried the burden of these cultural colonization
efforts.

In the anthologies of German literature used in Kafka's
Gymnasium, the genre of prose was somewhat neglected in
favor of drama and poetry (Wagenbach 1958, 52). The
function of prose was considered primarily expository, as in
scientific or historical essays. Even fiction was characterized
as the "representation of real deeds and events" (Wagenbach
1958, 52), and the main criterion for excellence here was the
clarity and precision of the description, i.e., full compliance
with the classical ideal. These were the standards Kafka was
taught and they are undoubtedly reflected in his style.
However, most German writers of the twentieth century
learned to write in a *Gymnasium* or a *Lyceum*, yet did not
feel compelled to adopt Kafka's precision and purity of style.
In fact, many of his literary contemporaries (e.g., Gustav
Meyrink) in Prague preferred to write in a rather bombastic,
melodramatic style from which Kafka consciously kept away

(cf. Wagenbach 1958, 81; Brod 1962, 58).   Unlike Kraus, Kafka published no polemical outbursts in defense of the standards of classical German, but especially the language of his diaries and letters has in many places a distinct affinity with the typically classical, Latin-inspired intricacy of Kraus' prose.   And as Wagenbach points out, Kraus was the only one to express (albeit in an exaggerated form) a purism similar to Kafka's (Wagenbach 1958, 89).

Thus, this writer too, even though he never resorted to borrowing "obsolete idioms" from Goethe, stood under the sway of Weimar classicism.   As already discussed in the first chapter of this study, much has been written about the question whether Kafka had a firm command of German, or whether, due to his special linguistically isolated situation in Prague, he lacked a certain "ursprünglich sicheres Sprach-gefühl" (Wagenbach 1958, 90).[118]   His style has been de-scribed as awkward, monotonous and barren,[119] yet Tuchol-sky, as mentioned before, called Kafka's language the "beste klassische Deutsch unserer Zeit" and Herman Hesse praised its "meisterhafte, kluge, bewegliche Prosa."[120]

There also exists disagreement over the quality of the German spoken in Prague.   Mauthner called it a "papierenes Deutsch," alluding to its artificiality and lack of roots among the people of that city (cf. also Wagenbach 1958, 83).[121]   But Johannes Urzidil, who grew up in Prague like Mauthner, maintains that the Prague intellectuals wrote as they spoke— "reines Hochdeutsch."[122]   Undoubtedly, both accounts have much truth in them.   The German spoken by the educated middle-class Jewry in Prague was indeed lacking the color and "melody"[123] of dialects.   Like Kafka, Mauthner regarded dialects as the only truly living part of a language and his lament "Ich besitze in meinem innern Sprachleben nicht die Kraft und die Schönheit einer Mundart" could have been uttered by Kafka.[124]   Yet the standards of the language of Weimar classicism, kept alive and transmitted through the humanistic schools of a culture-conscious Jewish middle class, shaped the German used by the Prague intellectuals so that they were quite justified in claiming that they were speaking and writing pure High German. As pointed out by J. Marchand, the fact that these intellectuals missed a sense of roots in their language, was closely connected with their overconscientious observation of its rules, the latter being an expression of the former.[125]

But for Kafka, the fact that one was capable of producing perfectly correct German sentences did not seem enough, for these sentences remained strange property "auch wenn nicht der einzigste Sprachfehler nachgewiesen werden könnte." The question of linguistic competence did not touch Kafka's problem, and neither do discussions of whether there are "Slavisms" or traces of Czech in his German (cf. Wagenbach 1958, 84, 90).[126] That Kafka consulted the Grimm dictionary (Brod 1962, 153) certainly does not set him apart from other German writers and can hardly explain his feelings of literary illegitimacy. However, behind his metaphor of the Gipsy literature with its stolen German child lies a certain view of the world and an aesthetic orientation closely connected with that view.

4

"Freundchen, ergieß dich!"
Kafka's Aesthetics

On November 5th 1915, that is, in the second year of the
First World War, whose events are rarely mentioned in his
diary, Kafka records that he spent an entire afternoon trying
to decide how many war bonds he should buy (T 486).
Calculating "feverishly" the interest, walking through the
"busiest" streets of Prague, he gradually slips into a mood of
creative inspiration. It is one of the few times Kafka expresses an emotional reaction to the war: "Ich fühlte mich
unmittelbar am Krieg beteiligt . . . " (T 486). However, he
has not suddenly turned into an amateur war profiteer, for the
interest he might "one day" (T 486) be able to collect, would
represent the way out of his present existence. He would be
able to quit his job as *Conzipist* (A 133) of the *Arbeiter-
Unfall-Versicherungsgesellschaft*, move out of Prague and
spend all his time writing . . . (cf. T 120, 266; 351, 436,
447, 451, 454, 456, 461, 489; Br 382; F 78, 125, 153, 170,
250, 408, 412, 645 f.; M 208). These kinds of thoughts lie
behind his "feverish" calculations and they naturally lead to
writing. He has a sudden sense of confidence in his ability

to write and begins excitedly to plan a writing schedule for the nights that would next be available to him (T 486). He experiences nervous heart pains (which were diagnosed as "Herzneurose" in 1916) (F 653), as he often does at the thought of not being able to find the necessary time to write. He feels, as he says, "das schon so oft erfahrene Unglück des verzehrenden Feuers, das nicht ausbrechen darf" (T 486) and to soothe his mounting anxiety, he begins a rhythmic chant: " . . . ich . . . erfand, um mich auszudrücken und zu beruhigen, den Spruch 'Freundchen, ergieß dich,' sang ihn unaufhörlich nach einer besonderen Melodie und begleitete den Gesang, indem ich ein Taschentuch in der Tasche wie einen Dudelsack immer wieder drückte und losließ" (T 486-87).

This episode encapsulates the frustrations and dilemmas of the writer Kafka. His meditative-ecstatic methods of writing are well-known and epitomized by the way he wrote his story "Das Urteil"—without interruption, in one night.[127] It was just because he was dependent on his visionary inspirations, inspirations that would only come to him after hours of solitude, that he devised his special schedule of sleeping in the afternoon and writing at night, which he describes as a "Kriegsdienst" in a letter to Milena (M 208; cf. Brod 1962, 100). The coveted results of such service, the pouring out of a good story like "Das Urteil," did not come often, for "die eigentliche Beute steckt doch erst in der Tiefe der Nacht in der zweiten, dritten, vierten Stunde." And he would need at least a half a year of working in this way "um mir erst 'die Zunge zu lösen'" (M 208).

The "Kriegsdienst" did not do for Kafka what he hoped, for it forced him to go to his office exhausted after only a few (or even no) hours of sleep, and he could never keep it up for very long. It was, according to Brod, the "Verstrickung in den Brotberuf" that brought about Kafka's increasing suffering and eventual sickness and death (Brod 1962, 113).

Many writers, perhaps the majority of them, have to, and are able to maintain some kind of work to support themselves. Some are destroyed by the tensions of their double existence, as for example J.M.R. Lenz (1751-1792), whose tragic career as a playwright, frustrated and ultimately destroyed by his "Verstrickung in den Brotberuf," has moved the imagination of several German writers.[128] Others managed quite well, as for example Gottfried Benn (1886-1956) and Alfred Döblin (1878-1957), both practicing physicians, and still others, like Thomas Mann (1875-1955), were able to live on the income generated by their writing. Most twentieth-century writers have to "muddle through" in some way, hoping for generous publishers, grants, editing or teaching positions to give them both living support and the time to write. Kafka, too, faced this problem, but in his case the solution had a disastrous effect on his life and his writing: he died still a young man (age forty-two) and his oeuvre remained slim. Given his dependence on inspirations, on images which could only come to him in an atmosphere of complete solitude and seclusion, Kafka was particularly disadvantaged by having to divide his life between "Brot-arbeit" and writing. For he rarely found enough time to develop fully his visions.

He feared these visions as much as he longed for them, for they would overwhelm him in times of inspiration with such a wealth of "Gutes" that he found himself unable to choose deliberately and was forced instead to grasp "blindly" and "at random" from the stream released in his imagination (T 162). As a result, the (arbitrarily) chosen and therefore weak images would lose all life and luster once written down, feeble in comparison to the imaginative wealth from which they came and incapable of conjuring it up again.

It is interesting that Kafka does not blame the inadequacy of language for his writing problem here, although the conclusion that words just don't capture the visions might easily have suggested itself to him. Instead he blames himself, his inability to produce anything but a random selection from the flood of images in his mind. Were he able to chose more deliberately, his writing would retain the life and luster of its original inspiration. Although he does not say so explicitly, his explanation for his artistic failure seems to imply that success in his case will be a matter of being able to make the right choices. As already discussed in Chapter Two, "right" and "wrong" play an important role in Kafka's poetics. The "right" images will lead to the kind of story that carries its final organization from the outset within itself, whereas the "wrong" ones exhaust what little strength they have merely by appearing (T 217). In another entry in his diary, Kafka gives a striking description of the feeling of writing something "wrong": "Dieses Gefühl des Falschen, das ich beim Schreiben habe, ließe sich unter dem Bild darstellen, daß einer vor zwei Bodenlöchern auf eine Erscheinung wartet, die nur aus dem zur rechten Seite herauskommen darf. Während aber gerade diese unter einem matt sichtbaren Verschluß bleibt, steigt aus dem linken eine Erscheinung nach der andern, sucht den Blick auf sich zu ziehen und erreicht dies schließlich mühelos durch ihren wachsenden Umfang, der endlich sogar die richtige Öffnung, so sehr man abwehrt, verdeckt" (T 216-217).

There is a great abundance of "wrong" images, which disappear as quickly as they appear, yet "one" (i.e., Kafka) continues watching in the hope that eventually the stream will exhaust itself and "true" images will begin to rise (T 217). Even the picture of the two holes that was to illustrate the feeling of writing something wrong, strikes Kafka as wrong: "Wie wenig kräftig ist das obere Bild. Zwischen tatsächliches Gefühl und vergleichende Beschreibung ist wie ein Brett eine zusammenhangslose Voraussetzung eingelegt" (T 217). This remark might well be interpreted as voicing a fundamental skepticism toward language, which, with its mere "pictures" (cf. also T 553), cannot adequately communicate the feeling he is trying to describe. But his comment may also be taken to express dissatisfaction with this *particular* metaphor, which seems weak to him and incapable of touching that feeling. The first interpretation would imply that Kafka thought *nothing* he (or anyone else) could ever write would truly depict a thought or a feeling.

According to Kessler Kafka believed just this, and therefore presents the reader with uninterpretable texts which point out through their very uninterpretability the fundamentally inadequate nature of language.[129] But the "Rätselcharakter"[130] of Kafka's stories could be understood differently. It might be said, for example, that Kafka depicted a truth about life which could only be expressed through mystifying pictures, i.e., not through the kind of philosophical considerations that according to Kessler are underlying Kafka's poetics. This last interpretation would in no way conflict with his concepts of "right" and "wrong," "true," "alive," etc., whereas it is hard to reconcile such concepts with the attitude of fundamental skepticism Kessler ascribes to Kafka. For if nothing can truly be expressed, in what sense are the pictures used by the author "right" or "wrong"?[131]

Yet these are the two basic categories underlying Kafka's poetics. The right words can conjure up the magnificence of life (T 544). The wrong words are wrong for specific reasons and could therefore, at least theoretically, be made right. There are many passages in Kafka's diaries and letters in which he discusses the merits and flaws of literary works, and his criticisms imply, as Hartmut Binder has demonstrated, basic principles of unity: unity of the atmosphere of a narrative, of the development of plot, of the character and the environment in which this character appears, of the overall perspective from which a story is told, all of which is to have a unified and concentrated impact on the reader.[132]

However, it wold be wrong to conclude from this that

Kafka had a rigid set of aesthetic rules. Consider the following: "Am Werk wird der Schriftsteller nachgeprüft; stimmt es, so ist es gut; ist es in einer schönen oder melodischen Nichtübereinstimmung, ist es auch gut; ist es aber in einer sich reibenden Nichtübereinstimmung, ist es schlecht" (Br 240). Even incongruity can be "right," just as long as it is not jarring. An example of such jarring incongruity is represented by some of the sentences Brod puts into the mouth of the figures in his sketch "Zirkus auf dem Land."[133] These figures represent a group of young men, presumably Brod and his friends, at the time (1909) in their mid-twenties, on an excursion into the countryside. Brod lets them utter certain phrases like "Die Villen dieser Nacht" which must have seemed to Kafka stilted, self-consciously lyrical (the notorious poetic genitive!) and therefore incongruous coming from the hikers: " . . . das haben die Freunde in der Geschichte nicht gesagt, glaube ich; wenn man sie zerreißt, haben sie das nicht gesagt" (Br 70).

Instead, Kafka preferred the simple and down-to-earth: "Am besten hat mir gefallen: 'Er suchte noch ein Steinchen, fand es aber nicht. Wir eilten u.s.w.'" (Br 70).   Kafka's initial, youthful attraction to "big words" (cf. Brod 1962, 75) and his subsequent efforts to eliminate all pretentious language from his writing have, as already mentioned, been described by Wagenbach (Wagenbach 1958, 104 f.). In an unpublished letter to his friend Oskar Pollak from the year 1902, Kafka apologizes for the poor quality of his early writing, the "Kindergekritzel," of which he is sending him a few samples. "Du mußt aber daran denken, daß ich in einer Zeit anfing, in der man 'Werke schuf', wenn man Schwulst schrieb; es gibt keine schlimmere Zeit zum Anfang. Und ich war so vertollt in die großen Worte" (Brod 1962, 75). By the time Kafka befriended Brod, he had already found his own artistic direction. This emerges from the first extended conversation between the two (in the winter of 1902-1903) reported by Brod, in the course of which a certain metaphor used by Gustav Meyrink (1868-1932) in the story "Der violette Tod" was discussed (Brod 1962, 57 f.). In this story Meyerink describes some butterflies by comparing them to "large opened books of magic," an image greatly admired by Brod, but rejected by Kafka as "far-fetched" and "gaudy." Brod describes: " . . . was effektvoll und intellektuell, künstlich und erdacht anmutete, verwarf er (wobei er aber nie derartig katalogisierende Worte anwandte). In ihm war etwas (und das liebte er auch an andern) von der 'leise redenden Stimme der Natur,' die Goethe ansprach. Als Gegenbeispiel, als das, was ihm gefiel, zitierte Kafka einen Passus von Hofmannsthal: 'Der Geruch nasser Steine in einem Hausflur.' Und er schwieg lange, setzte nichts hinzu, als müsse dieses Heimliche, Unscheinbare für sich selbst sprechen" (Brod 1962, 59).

Brod emphasizes repeatedly Kafka's preference for the simple and natural, because he wants to combat a certain understanding of the writer as drawn to the "Interessant-Angekränkelte, Bizarre, Groteske" (Brod 1962, 51) and the "aus Prinzip Schauerliche" (Brod 1962, 164; cf also 52, 59, 63, 82, 96). Given the eerie atmosphere and events of Kafka's fiction, such an understanding seems to suggest itself forcefully. In the face of stories like "Die Verwandlung," "Ein Landarzt," "Die Strafkolonie" it is hard to think of Kafka as possessing "delight in everything healthy and growing" (Brod 1962, 63) or an inclination toward "everything natural, simple and childlike fresh, full of striving for joy, happiness, decency, physical as well as spiritual strength" (Brod 1962, 164). Brod's angry assertion: "Kafkaesk ist das, was Kafka nicht war" (Brod, Prager Kreis 84) seems to deny the very essence of what countless readers have found in the dark world of his work. This may account for the fact that today Brod's understanding of his friend is often considered inadequate or at least extremely one-sided.

Brod, many critics feel, simply did not appreciate the absolute depth of Kafka's pessimism.[134]

It seems improbable that Kafka could have put up with a friend so fundamentally blind to the way he himself saw the world. And the fact that the deepest and most spiritual letters from the last years of his life are almost all addressed to Brod indicates that Kafka, on the contrary, felt he could count on certain fundamental conceptions concerning the world to be shared by his friend. Brod does not deny the dark view Kafka takes of modern life, but wants to emphasize that this view represents only part of Kafka's total vision of the world. The rest of this vision, Brod urges, should therefore not be ignored, especially since according to his opinion it constitutes Kafka's "decisive word": "Was ich betone und was . . . meine Darstellung Kafkas von anderen Darstellungen . . . unterscheidet, ist die Tatsache, daß ich das Positive, Lebensfreundliche . . . und im Sinn eines rechten erfüllten Lebens Religiöse, nicht aber Selbstverlorenheit, Lebensabgekehrtheit, Verzweiflung, 'tragische Position' für sein entscheidendes Wort halte" (Brod 1962, 207).

There are many passages both in Kafka's diaries and in his letters supporting Brod's claims. There are, for example, the enthusiastic entries about the Yiddish theater company, the affectionate descriptions of eastern Jewish figures, the delight over the "gesunde, fröhliche blauäugige Kinder" (Br 435) in the Jewish summer camp on the Baltic Sea in 1922 (cf. Br 435 ff.). He describes these children as "Ostjuden, durch Westjuden vor der Berliner Gefahr gerettet," and they certainly seem to represent to him the "striving for joy, happiness, decency and physical as well as spiritual strength" that according to Brod was so important to Kafka (Br 436).

The notion underlying both his love for openly ethnic Jewry and his despair over his own misspent life as a "western Jew" (cf. M 247) is indeed one of a "right and fulfilled life" (cf. also Brod 1962, 122). According to Brod Kafka often quoted a remark by Flaubert, who had remained single and childless for the sake of literature, but said of a family with several children he visited shortly before his death "Ils sont dans le vrai" (Brod 1962, 122). Such a life, it seemed to Kafka, required that one had roots in the world, raised a family (cf. H 209 f.) and wrote literature in the "light of the sun" (Br 384). In two letters from 1922, he uses the picture of "moving into one's house" (Br 385) to describe what he felt he should have done. Instead of "admiring and decorating" this house (Br 385) and thus abandoning it to "all powers of evil" (Br 386), he says, he should have lived in it. And he describes his homeless situation: "Ich bin von zuhause fort und muß immerfort nachhause schreiben, auch wenn alles Zuhause längst fortgeschwommen sein sollte in die Ewigkeit. Dieses ganze Schreiben ist nichts als die Fahne des Robinson auf dem höchsten Punkt der Insel" (Br 392). As this remark shows, Kafka felt that all his writing had a basic orientation which might be described metaphorically as directed "homeward." And even if "home," sadly, proved to be something lost to him forever, it nevertheless represented a deeply positive spiritual ideal against which he measured his own and all life.

His writing, too, should reflect this ideal in some sense, and his poetics of "right" and "wrong," "true" and "alive" will have to be looked at in this light. Since these terms are very general, it is not easy to develop a good sense of what role they played in Kafka's thinking. A more detailed picture of his artistic reactions, attitudes and values needs to be drawn to show this role. From such a picture will emerge the outlines of certain patterns that have already shown themselves in Kafka's relation to Yiddish and German and the cultural context surrounding these languages. They are the inclination to think of the world as an organism rather than a mechanism (an inclination that was so characteristic for Herder and Goethe),[135] in which human beings, the for Herder and Goethe),[135] in which human beings, the language they speak, the art they create, their culture and their lives are all intricately connected with each other, the way the different parts of a biological organism are connected.

In keeping with the biological picture, the notion of an organic order of the world brings with it the concepts of natural growth and roots. The *Weltanschauung* behind this metaphoric language represents, as already discussed in Chapter Two, a major trend of thought in the history of European culture.[136] It was embodied in German literature by figures like Herder, Goethe, Novalis and others and continued into the twentieth century by a number of thinkers and writers (Dilthey, Wittgenstein),[137] among whom Karl Kraus through his *Fackel* became the most vocal representative. It is illuminating to review briefly some of Kraus' remarks about language and poetry, for they show an affinity with Kafka's views and therefore help to identify them.

Kafka, for example, complains that in his own writing ideas don't come to him "von der Wurzel aus," but instead only from "irgendwo gegen ihre Mitte" (T 12), and that no word comes to him "vom Ursprung her," but instead "weit am Wege irgendwo, zufällig . . . festgepackt" (F 341). The aesthetic concepts of "roots" and "origin" also play a central role in Kraus' understanding of language. As previously noted, he criticizes Heine's wit for its "rootlessness" (KW VIII 208), for Heine remains on the surface of language, whereas the true artist receives his inspiration from the profoundest sources: "Alles Geschaffene bleibt, wie es da war, eh es geschaffen wurde. Der Künstler holt es als Fertiges vom Himmel herunter." Access to a (vaguely platonic) realm of "preformed thoughts" (KW VIII 205) thus becomes for Kraus the essence of poetic creation. And such access cannot be achieved through deliberate, rationally controlled efforts, for the poet's language "tastet im Dunkel der Welt einem verlorenen Urbild nach" (KW III 338).

Kafka might well have agreed with this description, because for him too, writing represented—as already noted—a kind of blind search. In his case, it was the search for the "organisms" of stories whose hidden predetermined "organization" would eventually give them artistic "justification." Helplessly waiting for the "right" image to appear from a closed opening, blindly grasping from an overwhelming flood of images, Kafka, too, found himself "groping in the dark" for an "Urbild." He records in his diary the ecstatic experience of finding such a "proto image," that is, of writing "Das Urteil." The story "develops" in front of him, he "moves ahead in its waters," and "everything can be said" because there is a great fire in him, ready to transform "even the strangest ideas" (T 293). And he concludes: "*Nur so* kann geschrieben werden, nur in einem solchen Zusammenhang, mit solcher vollständigen Öffnung des Leibes und der Seele" (T 294).

A few months later, he describes the writing of "Das Urteil" in terms of giving birth: " . . . die Geschichte ist wie eine regelrechte Geburt mit Schmutz und Schleim aus mir herausgekommen . . . " (T 296). This picture corresponds strikingly to Kraus' view that the "schöpferische Mensch nur ein erwähltes Gefäß ist" (KW VIII 189). Such metaphoric descriptions of artistic creation suggest a sense of passivity on the part of the artist, of being dependent on receiving inspiration "from above." Kafka expresses this sense when he speaks of his writing as the "Erlaubnis im Dienst-zusein," over which he has as little control as over the outpourings of his imagination (M 208). Given this lack of control, "right" and "wrong," for Kafka, have to become largely a matter of intuition. The "organic" character of a story will (or will not) emerge gradually as it is written, but it cannot be brought about through deliberate manipulation. In fact, any self-conscious attempts at construction were consistently comments on the poems of Gottfried Kölwel (1889-1958).[138] Kafka praises Kölwel's poetry for its "good and true" qualities but criticizes its occasional "kühle Gefühlswendung," which seems to him as though "performed on the trapeze" instead of "in the heart" (Br 154). Especially the poem "Trostgesang" contains two very visible "Stützbalken" which give away the abstract design behind the otherwise good poem. These "beams" consist in two rather awkward three-line passages which represent parallel constructions except for the first word of each line, which changes from "furchtbar" to "Versöhnung":

> Furchtbar, wie da jeder Bettler steht!
> Furchtbar, wie da jeder Kranke fleht!
> Furchtbar, wie da jedes Auge sich zum Sterben dreht!

and:

> Versöhnung, wie da der Bettler steht?
> Versöhnung, wie da der Kranke fleht?
> Versöhnung, wie sich das Auge zum Sterben dreht?[139]

The turn from despair to hope represents the theme of the poem, but since its expression here consists in an artificial construction that does not come "from the heart," the poem's organism seems flawed to Kafka.

The opposite of such artificial poetic constructions were for Kafka the ideas and images that came to his imagination spontaneously and without conscious deliberation.[140] These images could, once they were there, only be chosen or rejected by him, depending on whether they possessed the kind of "inner truth" he saw in "Das Urteil" (F 156), or were only "Machwerk" like the "two or three pages" before the end of the "Strafkolonie" (Br 159). Kafka never was able to correct the flawed passage and eventually had to take it out altogether.[141]   For, as Binder points out, it was nearly impossible for him to make any significant changes or corrections once the original inspiration had been written down.   His manuscripts reflect this in that they begin at the beginning and continue uninterruptedly till the end (or the breaking off) of the story.[142]   Once the spontaneous flow of his imagination had stopped, the "right" words were no longer available.   This is strikingly illustrated by two diary entries of the year 1914.   On December 19th, he writes: "Gestern den 'Dorfschullehrer' fast bewußtlos geschrieben, fürchtete mich aber, länger als dreiviertel zwei zu schreiben, die Furcht war begründet, ich schlief fast gar nicht . . . und war dann im Bureau in entsprechendem Zustand" (T 449).   A week later, he notes: "Heute abend fast gar nichts geschrieben und vielleicht nicht mehr imstande, den 'Dorfschullehrer' fortzusetzen, an dem ich jetzt fast eine Woche arbeitete und den ich gewiß in drei freien Nächten rein und ohne äußerliche Fehler fertiggebracht hätte, jetzt hat er, trotzdem er noch fast am Anfang ist, schon zwei unheilbare Fehler in sich und ist außerdem verkümmert" (T 451; cf. also T 436, 447).   In the end, he abandoned the story (T 454).   Similarly, after he had been working for some time on his novel *Amerika*, which he himself sometimes called *Der Verschollene*,[143] he foresaw grave problems with its eventual revision: "Was für eine schwere Arbeit, vielleicht eine unmögliche das sein wird, nach der ersten Beendigung in die toten Partien auch nur ein halbes Leben zu bringen! Und wieviel Unrichtiges wird stehen bleiben müssen, weil dafür keine Hilfe aus der Tiefe kommt" (F 251).   Kafka often preferred not appearing in print to having to revise his stories.   Thus when Brod urges him to prepare his first collection of prose pieces for publication, he complains bitterly about the "verdammte Sichzwingen" and the "künstliche Arbeit" involved in the revisions (Br 99).   The fact that spontaneity was such an absolute prerequisite for his writing is reflected in his poetics.

Works have to be "pure" (T 111, 129, 345, 451; Br 96, 102, 154, 396; F 160; M 208) in the sense of being free of artificiality and without any traces of deliberate design or "mechanische Phantasie" (T 331, 339, 375, 435, 463; Br 70, 71, 159, 185, 192, 213). And works have to be "alive" (Br 21, 94, 111, 247, 313, 315 f., 416, 423) in the sense of having grown in a way that is natural (T 38, 236; F 125, 186) and "notwendig" (Br 214).

In this light, Kafka criticizes the ending of a novel by his friend Oskar Baum because it is "not right" for a "Geschichte, die sich so ruhig heraufgearbeitet hat und hier mit einem Ruck ein Stückchen zurück in ein ungesundes Dunkel geschoben wird. Was hat Ihnen denn der Leser getan . . . " (Br 71). The end, a monologue, is deliberately designed to disrupt the flow of the story, which had up to that point gradually established a certain depth, the "Tiefe der Geschichte" (Br 70). Abruptly cutting off the reader's involvement in the story, sometimes described as destroying the reader's illusion of real life, is a familiar literary device. By reminding the reader that he is, after all, just reading a novel (or watching a play), the author can direct his attention to other important features of the work. (Tieck's *Gestiefelter Kater* and many of Brecht's plays represent good examples of such deliberate intervention by the author.)[144]

Kafka did not approve of this device and criticizes it elsewhere in connection with one of Hamsun's works (Br 68), in which a character comments on his own puzzling role in the story, thus disrupting, in Kafka's view, the hold that story has on the reader's imagination. The comment, he says, " . . . ist doch eine Stelle, wo die Geschichte in der Gegenwart des Lesers sich selbst zerstört oder wenigstens verdunkelt, nein verkleinert, entfernt, so daß der Leser, um sie nicht zu verlieren, in die offenbare Umzingelung hineingehen muß" (Br 68). It is not hard to see why Kafka rejected this kind of "alienation effect." A story represented for him a natural organism to be developed by its author according to its innate laws.   Deliberately disrupting its impact on the reader had to seem to him a mechanical and artificial device.   The reader, Kafka thought, had to be led to deeper and deeper involvement with the story.   Just as its author, one might add, first had to submerge himself more and more profoundly in its writing.   Only through such intense submersion, it seems, could the natural organization of the story be developed by Kafka or in his view be appreciated by the reader.   The author, he felt, should avoid anything that might interfere with this appreciation.

It is for this reason that Kafka rejected self-conscious moves "on the trapeze," such as the mechanical conception of a poem or the deliberate disruption of a story.   Such artificial devices could only lessen the reader's appreciation and had for him no place in the natural organism of the literary work.   Based on intellectual considerations they simply did not come from the author's heart.   Kafka's metaphor of good writing as coming "from the heart" (T 377) must not be misinterpreted as expressing a preference for emotionally charged literature such as Goethe's *Die Leiden des jungen Werthers*, which seemed to him full of "Gemütsschwefel" (Br 25).   Kafka's own writing, including "Das Urteil," a story which he approved of almost without reservation, is marked by its strikingly unemotional tone.[145]   Literature "from the heart," it seems, cannot be equated with emotional outpourings.   The question is therefore, how are we to understand this metaphor?

To answer this question it may be helpful to look at an example of the kind of text that for Kafka came "from the heart."   There are numerous comments on literary works in his letters and diaries.   These comments are mostly marked by their (in a negative sense) critical character.   As he said himself, he could find some flaw in the works of even the greatest writers (F 292), and he viewed his own stories with a mercilessly critical eye (T 104, 142, 161 f., 192, 331, 377, 444, 463; Br 23, 85, 111, 115, 159, 216; F 180 f.). The rare instance of a literary composition finding Kafka's wholehearted approval is therefore especially interesting and may help to provide a better sense of what he meant by "from the heart." The poem "Nun leb wohl, du kleine Gasse" by Albert Graf von Schlippenbach (1800-1886), which was set to music and, like his "Ein Heller und ein Batzen," became a popular German song, represents such a composition. It is interesting that A. Mosbeck, the editor of a collection of Schlippenbach's poems, characterizes these poems as "a kind of late romantic wave" appearing in a "time to which it has already grown unfamiliar." "Nun leb wohl . . ." has indeed the "fresh, naive"[146] quality of a folk song and does seem to belong to an earlier era when such songs were collected (and written) by writers like Herder, Arnim and others, who had discovered the power of folkloric literature and were inspired by it:

Nun leb wohl, du kleine Gasse,
Nun ade, du stilles Dach!
Vater, Mutter sahn mir traurig,
Und die Liebste sah mir nach.

Hier in weiter Ferne,
Wie's mich nach der Heimat zieht!
Lustig singen die Gesellen,
Doch es ist ein falsches Lied.

Andre Städtchen kommen freilich,
Andre Mädchen zu Gesicht;
Ach wohl sind es andre Mädchen,
Doch die eine ist es nicht.

Andre Städtchen, andre Mädchen,

Ich da mittendrin so stumm!
Andre Mädchen, andre Städtchen,
O, wie gerne kehrt ich um.

Kafka learned the song while he was staying at a health
spa in 1912, where he sang it with the other guests in the
mornings (F 103). He "fell in love" with the song and
copied it for himself, even though he could only remember
its melody "as a sigh" (F 103). He praised its "simple
purity" in a letter to Brod (Br 102), and sent his treasured
copy of it to Felice Bauer, urging her to be sure to return it
(F 103). The song, he tells Felice, combines "vollständige
Ergriffenheit" with a simple yet perfect structure: " . . .
jede Strophe besteht aus einem Ausruf und dann einer
Neigung des Kopfes" (F 103). In other words, the poem has
for Kafka the character of a simple yet extremely expressive
gesture, for in all its simplicity it conveys a deep sadness
that, as Kafka assures Felice, is entirely "truthful" (F 103).
This genuine and strong feeling is expressed not through
well-chosen, artistic language, but rather in plain, even
repetitious words arranged into a "completely regular"
structure (F 103).

But unlike the "Stützbalken" in Kölwel's poem, which
had been erected as part of an artificial construction and
seemed to Kafka like moves "on the trapeze," the regular
pattern of Schlippenbach's song pleased him by its very
regularity. It suggested to him two natural and basic human
gestures, two wordless expressions of sadness that are
familiar to every human being: crying out in grief and
lowering the head in sorrow. These gestures, like all spontaneous gestures, come truly "from the heart." They are
neither deliberate nor thought out. But they can communicate
more powerfully than words, for when we see them we know
immediately what they mean. If a poem strikes Kafka as a
gesture, it is communicating its feeling to him in a similar

way, directly, spontaneously, from heart to heart. And this, one might say, represents his artistic ideal.

"Das Urteil" came very close to this ideal. Its "inner truth," Kafka says, has to be "admitted anew again and again by each reader" (F 156). Like a lyrical poem, the story was written with "complete opening up of body and soul" (T 294; cf. also T 268, 336 and F 103 for Kafka's concept of creative "Ergriffenheit," total emotional involvement in writing) and like a poem it requires an intense personal response from each individual reader. The story communicates not so much through its words as, in a manner of speaking, through its gestures. It may be relevant in this connection that Kafka did not want its figures to be understood as "real people" (F 396). The friend, he suggests to Felice, may represent "was dem Vater und Georg gemeinsam ist" or "vielleicht der perspektivische Wechsel der Beziehungen zwischen Vater und Sohn" (F 397). As emerges from two letters negotiating the publication of the story, Kafka thought of it as "mehr Gedicht als Erzählung" (Br 148), "mehr gedichtmäßig als episch" (Br 149), and requested that it be printed by itself, for like a poem, it needed to be surrounded by "freien Raum" (Br 148).

Kafka's view of his story need not dictate our understanding of it, but that he saw it in this way tells us something about his poetics. For him, the literary work had to be alive and pure in the same sense a gesture is alive and pure. He was struck by flaws such as pretentious language among hiking friends or artificial constructions in poetry in the same way one might be struck by a self-conscious, awkward motion breaking off an initially graceful gesture. He detected such flaws almost everywhere: "Ich meine nämlich, selbst jedes höchste Literaturwerk hat ein Schwänzchen der Menschlichkeit, welches, wenn man will und ein Auge dafür hat, leicht zu zappeln anfängt und die Erhabenheit und Gottähnlichkeit des Ganzen stört" (F 292). But he seems to have discovered no such "little tail" in Schlippenbach's poem. With its simple, folk song-like structure it represented to him a perfectly controlled artistic expression of genuine feeling.   He saw no traces of self-consciousness or artificiality in it, no awkward seams between content and form.   In the sense, perhaps, that a gesture can be said to *be* the emotion it expresses, for Kafka, the song's form (i.e., each stanza's outcry and "lowering of the head") *was* its content (i.e., the sad longing for home).   Form and content had become one as they do in a spontaneous gesture.   Kafka wanted all his writing to have the character of spontaneous gestures and to communicate as these do, directly from heart to heart.

That Kafka sometimes looked at his writing as more or less successful gesturing, is shown by a description he gives of himself as having to write like someone who is so agitated that he can only express himself by waving his arms about wildly (T 180).   This view, closely connected with the kind of person he was and the way he wrote, has important implications for his feelings about the language he used to create his stories.   This language sometimes came to him in a way that made him feel he could say everything.   His "besondere Art der Inspiration," he notes in his diary, is that he "alles kann" (T 41 f.).   For example, he only had to write down a sentence like "Er schaute aus dem Fenster" for it to be at once perfect (T 42).   In connection with "Das Urteil," too, he felt that "alles gesagt werden kann" (T 293).

His most explicit positive statement about language appears in a letter to Felice.   In a previous letter, he had told her that, given his inability to have any real relationship with her, he should really keep away from her.   Now he was trying to take back the bitter words and assure her that "falsche Sätze" had forced themselves into his writing by clinging to his pen and being "in die Briefe mitgeschleift" (F 305).   But he asks Felice to love him in spite of these cruel sentences whose words were "hervorgetrieben" out of him in a "geheim sich vollziehenden Weg" and have produced, after all, self-knowledge as well as heartache (F 306). In this sense, the "wrong" sentences are really not "wrong," and, in general, Kafka says, claims about the inadequacy and limitations of language are "ganz verfehlt": "Ich bin nicht der Meinung, daß einem die Kraft fehlen kann, das, was man sagen oder schreiben will, auch vollkommen auszudrücken. Hinweise auf die Schwäche der Sprache und Vergleiche zwischen der Begrenztheit der Worte und der Unendlichkeit des Gefühls sind ganz verfehlt. Das unendliche Gefühl bleibt in den Worten genau so unendlich, wie es im Herzen war. Das was im Innern klar ist, wird es auch unweigerlich in Worten. Deshalb muß man niemals um die Sprache Sorge haben, aber im Anblick der Worte oft Sorge um sich selbst" (F 306). A few weeks later, in despair over the difficulties he is having with writing, he expresses reservations with regard to this optimistic statement: "Als ich im vollen Schreiben war, schrieb ich Dir einmal, daß jedes wahre Gefühl die zugehörigen Worte nicht sucht, sondern mit ihnen zusammenstößt oder gar von ihnen getrieben wird. Vielleicht ist es so doch nicht ganz wahr" (F 341). But as though to quiet his own doubts, he adds that even with "a firm hand" he could not achieve all he wants in writing to Felice, since he is trying to convince her that she should both love him and hate him (F 341).

Kafka did think that language had certain fundamental limitations, and these thoughts will be discussed in the next chapter, which will deal with the philosophical dimensions of such a view. The two quoted passages, on the other hand, can hardly serve to prove that Kafka regarded language with profound skepticism. Yet Richard Thieberger cites them in his essay on Kafka and language, introducing a section which concludes that "the problem of language, the inadequacy of expression is made again and again the theme of "Kernstellen" in Kafka's writing.[147]   However, as the present study shows, his attitude toward language was much more complicated than such a description indicates. Kafka's recognition of the limitations of language cannot, as the next chapter will demonstrate, be equated with the kind of skeptical view taken, for example, by Mauthner in his *Beiträge zu einer Kritik der Sprache*.[148]   Kafka's thinking about language contains none of the radical (and highly theoretical) skepticism expressed by Mauthner, but has instead, as already discussed, considerable affinity with Kraus' views.

Kraus, defender of classical German, does not have much sympathy for writers complaining about the inadequacy of language, as was fashionable in Germany and especially Austria around the turn of the century.[149]   In response to Jakob Wassermann's complaint that language, as revenge for the abuses it has suffered, no longer serves the poets but has instead begun to confuse the minds of people, he writes scornfully: "Die Herren Dichter brauchen eine andere Sprache? Ich werde ihnen was malen; besser dichten sollen sie, dann wird's schon gehn! . . . Der große Maler muß auch mit Kot malen können . . . " (KW II 251 f.). Kraus' attitude is characteristic of the conservative trend of thinking of his time, a trend that held on to the traditional ideals of German literature as they had been set down by the great writers of its classical period, Lessing, Herder, Goethe and others.[150] To the extent that Kafka demanded "truth" and "purity" in artistic expression, the "natural" and the "alive," he shared these ideals and made them his own absolute standards. Kafka's love for "Nun leb wohl, du kleine Gasse" expresses the same spirit as Kraus' love for Liliencron's nature poetry, the same yearning for literature that is inspired by "the heart."

It was in this spirit that Kraus developed his peculiar language mysticism, and it was in this spirit that Kafka made statements about words being mysteriously forced out of him, colliding with his true feelings, even driving these feelings along before them. The spirit of these remarks seems to have little in common with Mauthner's picture of human beings who, when struck by an unfamiliar feeling, deliberately chose a word that they attach to it from then on.[151] Rather, Kafka's description brings to mind Kraus' conception of a living language whose heartbeat the poet can hear as he struggles to give new life to the "oldest word" (KW III 135). What makes the words alive for Kraus is that they are intuitively found: "Die Sprache hat in Wahrheit der, der nicht das Wort, sondern nur den Schimmer hat, aus dem er das Wort ersehnt, erlöst und empfängt." (KW III 328) In the regions of art, language "sleepwalks" more safely than when it "walks correctly" (i. e., according to grammatical rules) on the ground (KW II 119) Any renewal of language can therefore only come from poetry (KW II 19): "Jedes Wort ist ursprünglich ein Gedicht und was den Vollbegriff des Dings umfaßt, ist ihm nur abgelallt" (KW II 381). Every child according to Kraus would be equipped with "dichterische Kraft" had not this power atrophied under the influence of civilization (KW II 381). And he defines poetic power as the ability to form "Anschauungen zu Lautbildern" (KW II 381). Poetic power and the power to create new language are for Kraus, as for Herder and Vico, nearly identical, and both are derived from a source quite beyond human reason and rational deliberation. Words according to Kraus were originally forced on human beings by the things they encountered, and represented spontaneous responses to these things, similar to an exclamation or a smile.

Kafka never formulated such views and generally preferred describing language to theorizing about it. But the concepts involved in his poetics show a great deal of affinity with those involved in Kraus' understanding of language. Kraus describes the first uttering of a color word as a poetic creation inspired by the sight of the color. The first mouth to utter that word "could not do otherwise" (KW II 381). Kafka, too, as I have tried to show, felt that the language of his stories was drawn out of him in a compelling way. He depended on the creative outpourings of his imagination, without which he could not write and which he could not control, because they alone offered the promise of writing, at least sometimes, "from the heart."

5

Pictures and Parables
Kafka and the Limits of Language

Up to this point I have discussed a number of ways in which Kafka might be said to have had a problem with language. The historical and geographical conditions that shaped his culture and his relationship to that culture contributed importantly to these problems, as did the circumstances of his personal life, for example, his unhappy relationship with his father and his sense of exclusion from human society in general. As a writer, Kafka was frustrated by having to devote much of his time to the work at the *Arbeiter-Unfall-Versicherungsgesellschaft*, and was, one might say, ultimately defeated by his illness. Feeling alienated both from the literature and the language in which he wrote, he increasingly turned to what he must have considered his lost spiritual roots, Judaism, and in particular, the Hasidism of eastern Europe. It was in this context that there arose for him what might be called a philosophical problem with language.

What is meant by this will emerge in more detail in the following discussion of a remarkable analogy between Witt-

genstein's and Kafka's problem with language.[152]   Both
writers worried about the ineffectiveness of a certain kind of
language in the realm of ethics and aesthetics, and both came
to the conclusion that an altogether different language was
used to express this realm.   Kafka never articulated such
thoughts very explicitly, but his perspective emerges clearly
from his   preference for pictures and metaphors, which
comes out so strikingly in his remarks about language and in
his Zürau aphorisms, where he came perhaps closest to
"theorizing" about language.   In order to understand these
aphorisms, it is important to see them against the background
of that preference, as coming from a writer whose inspirations consisted in (sometimes overwhelming) streams of
pictures and who was quite aware of and struck by the
pictorial quality of his imagination.   He found that what he
wanted to say could be expressed best in pictures.   He came
to feel it could *only* be expressed in that way, and he formulated this view in the context of the aphorisms.   Wittgenstein's concern with language, too, involved the recognition of the "limits of language," the inability of discursive,
descriptive language to express the ethical and the aesthetic,
and the special role played by pictures in the kind of language actually used in that context.   Wittgenstein's thought
on this subject can, I believe, help to   illuminate Kafka's
remarks about language, for the Austrian philosopher made
explicit and elucidated the kind of perspective taken by his
contemporary from Prague.   This perspective will therefore
be discussed in conjunction with Wittgenstein's work, the
latter serving to make the former more accessible.

Throughout his life Kafka expressed in his diaries and
letters dissatisfaction with his ability to communicate as a
writer (T 37 f., 113, 161, 186 f., 324, 338, 465, 468, 514;
Br 90, 140, 235; F 149, 197, 234, 305, 355, 367, 381, 381,
448, 555; H 111; M 249).   He summarizes his misgivings in
a letter to Milena: " . . . ich suche immerfort etwas Nicht-

Mitteilbares mitzuteilen, etwas Unerklärliches zu erklären, von etwas zu erzählen, was ich in den Knochen habe und was nur in diesen Knochen erlebt werden kann" (M 249). He, as many before and after him, came to confront what is perhaps best characterized as the limits of language.[153] The things he felt "in his bones" could not be described adequately, for they were, as he says in a letter to Felice, "kaum in menschliche Worte zu übersetzende Dinge" (F 381).

He was struck by a certain incommensurability of the empirical world and "everything else": "Wunderbare, gänzlich widerspruchsvolle Vorstellung, daß einer, der zum Beispiel um drei Uhr in der Nacht gestorben ist, gleich darauf, etwa in der Morgendämmerung, in ein höheres Leben eingeht. Welche Unvereinbarkeit liegt zwischen dem sichtbar Menschlichen und allem anderen!" (T 338). And the more he tried to come to terms with "everything else," the "inner world" of the human soul (H 72), the more it seemed to elude his words.

An "inner law" demanding "unity" (presumably, Kafka was referring to marriage), seemed to have struck him inexplicably, unexpectedly, out of nowhere, and taken over his life. This "inner law" could not be communicated because it was "incomprehensible," but for that very reason it left him, like a dream, with the urge to tell about it (H 111 f.). When he sought to put into words his profoundest thoughts and feelings he experienced the limits of language most acutely. This final chapter will focus on Kafka's special concern with the difficulty of talking about the soul, the "inner world" (H 72), and the "mythical beyond" of spiritual salvation (E 328). He formulated this concern in what is now known as the "Zürau Aphorisms," his most philosophical work, which shows a remarkable affinity to the thoughts and even the style of Ludwig Wittgenstein.

As will be discussed in this chapter, Wittgenstein, too, had been struck as a young man by the limitations of language that were troubling Kafka. His view of the nature of these limitations was shaped by his work on the logical structure of language which ruled out the possibility of ethical statements. He found that all talk about the "inner world," that is, ethics and aesthetics, had to be excluded from "meaningful" language, because it could not fit its logical model. For Wittgenstein as for Kafka certain aspects of human experience could not be depicted properly with descriptive language. And yet Wittgenstein was not denying that ethical and artistic language can play a meaningful role in human life, as the last sentence of his *Tractatus* is sometimes misunderstood to be doing. He wanted to point out that *a certain way of talking* about ethics was meaningless, but not that ethical thought could never be expressed with words. Ethics and aesthetics, he might have said later, enter our language, but in a very different way from science.[154]

Kafka, too, was aware of a difference between the way words can be used to talk about what he called the "inner" and the "sensory world" (H 72, 92). And while both he and Wittgenstein felt that the "inner world" could not be talked about in the same way as, say, science, they nevertheless saw the possibility of expressing it within language, of, as it were, expressing the inexpressible. As the later Wittgenstein would have said, the grammar of ethical or aesthetic language is not the same as that of scientific language. Understanding one involves very different relationships and responses from understanding the other. In science, for example, it is important that all procedures reflect certain standards of objectivity and accuracy. This, in turn (among other factors), determines the kinds of things that are appropriate to do and to say, what to ask, when and how to disagree, what conclusions to draw, how to apply those conclusions, etc. Such standards of objectivity and accuracy generally do not play an important role in ethics or aesthetics, or rather what is counted as objective and accurate there is very different from what is considered objective and accurate in science.[155] A farmer praying for rain would not "evaluate" the "results" of his prayer the way a scientist evaluates the results of an experiment.   A drought would not be likely to lead the farmer to the conclusion that prayer is worthless (although it might), but if an experiment fails to produce certain results, the scientist will make immediate modifications or possibly abandon the experiment altogether.   If he did not, he would be considered incompetent.   A farmer, maintaining steadfast trust in God in spite of failed crops, may be deemed a fool by some, but will be admired, even envied for his spiritual strength by many others.   It is these kinds of factors that, as Wittgenstein would have put it later, determine the grammar of what is said and done in a scientific or ethical context.[156]

Kafka and Wittgenstein, having both been struck by the limitations of descriptive language with respect to the "inner world," attempted to define more closely the grammar of religious language, Kafka, the poet, in his aphorisms and his much-analyzed meta-parable "Von den Gleichnissen," Wittgenstein, the philosopher, in lectures, discussions and private notes.   Here too, as will emerge from the concluding portion of this chapter, there exists a striking affinity of thought between the two, all the more striking in that neither knew about the other's work.   This affinity might perhaps be described best as one of perspective and sensitivity.   It expressed itself in the way both of them were struck by the fact that accounts of the empirical world, those given by science, and empirical psychology in particular, could not provide explanations of or answers to ethical problems. Kafka was not, as was Wittgenstein, addressing certain traditional questions of western philosophy, and he did not formulate his concerns in terms of philosophical considerations, but rather as a poet through aphorisms and parables. And while Wittgenstein's work should be seen against the background of western philosophy, Kafka's aphorisms can be appreciated better in the context of eastern European Hasidism, its body of anecdotes and folklore, its preference for pictures and parables, its rejection of abstract speculations concerning matters of religion, its insistence on the expression of faith in the "here and now."[157]

In the early fall of 1917, Kafka found out that he had tuberculosis. Once he had been officially diagnosed, his life changed a great deal. He applied for retirement from the *Arbeiter-Unfall-Versicherungsgesellschaft* (he was turned down and was not retired by the company until July 1922), and broke off his second engagement with Felice Bauer. He moved away from Prague for the first time in his life and went to Zürau, a small west Bohemian town, to live with his youngest sister Ottla, who was working on a rural estate there as part of her agricultural training.[158] Even these rough outlines of the events show that the winter of 1917-1918 was a time of self-examination for Kafka. He no longer had to fight with himself over whether to get married or not, and he was, at least for some time (he stayed in Zürau for eight months),[159] free from his work at the office. He read Hasidic stories, with which he could always feel "at home," as he told Brod in a letter (Br 173), and he returned to his work on Jizchak Löwy's biography, for which he had taken many notes during conversations with the actor five years earlier (H 154-159).[160] He was impressed by the farmers whom he described as "Edelmänner, die sich in die Landwirtschaft gerettet haben" (T 535) and with country living in general: "Ordnung ist hier in Tag- und Jahreszeiten, und man kann sich ihr einfügen, es ist gut" (Br 231). He helped Ottla with some of her work, enjoyed gardening (Br 201, 233; H 107) and the farm animals (Br 202, 240), and began to read a great deal of Kierkegaard (cf. Br 190, 201, 224, 234, 236, 237 ff., 240 and H 112, 124 f., 444 f.).[161]

It was during these months in Zürau that Kafka wrote the aphorisms published after his death by Brod under the title

"Betrachtungen über Sünde, Leid, Hoffnung und den wahren Weg" (H 39-54). These aphorisms were originally written into notebooks (the "Oktavhefte") together with a few autobiographical notes and many fragmentary beginnings of stories, and then selected, numbered and copied into a manuscript by Kafka himself (cf. Brod's remarks, H 438). Brod's title, although probably not entirely faithful to Kafka's style, gives a good sense of what these aphorisms are about. After having shed most of the things that made up his life, i.e., having left behind, all at the same time, his great love affair, his work at his office, his life with his parents, even the "inner" Prague Circle, he was (a little like the members of a certain Russian sect, who throw away all earthly possessions on New Year's Day), free to turn his attention to the kinds of concerns he described as "tiefste Sorgen der geistigen Existenzbehauptung" (H 204) or "Sorgen der innersten Existenz" (T 229) or simply "die schreckliche Unsicherheit meiner innern Existenz" (T 304).

Presumably it was under the pressure of these kinds of cares that Kafka, already two years earlier, had visited with Brod and another friend, Georg alias Mordechai Langer, a "Wunderrabbi" in Prague. Langer, the son of a Prague liquor dealer (Br 142), was, according to Brod, a "western" Jew who had submerged himself in Hasidism and lived for years "at the court" of the most important Hasidic Rabbi at the time (Br 505; F 666).[162] "All rabbis are wild" he told Kafka and Brod who may have been somewhat startled by the appearance of the wonder rabbi, whose underpants could be glimpsed beneath his caftan, and who "reached into the food" with his fingers (T 478 f.). The rabbi struck Kafka as both "dirty and pure" and the encounter moved him to look at the Bible (T 479). As Brod reports, he and Kafka were taught Hebrew by Langer, who also introduced them to the "Sitten der chassidischen Welt" (Brod, *Prager Kreis* 98).[163] A few weeks after the visit, Kafka wrote down in his diary three of the Hasidic stories Langer told him (T 482 ff.).

A year later, in the summer of 1916 when Kafka was staying in Marienbad, he visited Langer, who at that time was living "at the court" of the Belz rabbi. In a long letter to Brod, Kafka described the experience of joining the rabbi's following of disciples on their daily evening walks (Br 141 ff.). Kafka's description is somewhat ironic. The rabbi's naive questions about the buildings they were passing, his "special eastern Jewish amazement" (Br 146) over, for example, the steam pipes leading to the steam bath (Br 145), struck Kafka primarily as funny. But the way in which Langer and the other followers expressed their complete devotion to the rabbi, finding "deeper meaning" in the most trivial details of each excursion (Br 145), observing with great care the rule of never walking in front of the rabbi, carrying behind him a chair, water and other objects he might suddenly need, all this seemed to Kafka to represent "Wahrheit" (Br 142) and "durchaus Gottesgnadentum" (Br 145). Clearly, no matter how ridiculous he found the actual details of their daily lives, Kafka was attracted by the disciples' "ruhiges glückliches Vertrauen" in their spiritual leader, by the commitment and the faith that held them all together (Br 144).

The distinct traces of Jewish mystical thought as expressed by the Hasidic tales of eastern Europe in Kafka's Zürau aphorisms as well as the short prose pieces he wrote around the same time, have already been noted by Emmy L. Kerkhoff in 1972 and by Werner Hoffmann in 1975, and more recently also by Karl Erich Grözinger and Marina Cavarocchi Arbib.[164] Kafka himself observes in 1922 that his works contain the tentative beginnings of a new "Geheimlehre," a new "Kabbala," but concludes that he did not have the strength for such a renewal: "Allerdings ein wie unbegreifliches Genie wird hier verlangt, das neue Wurzeln in die alten Jahrhunderte treibt oder die alten Jahrhunderte neu erschafft und mit all dem sich nicht ausgibt, sondern jetzt erst sich auszugeben beginnt" (T 553). There is no question about the deeply religious nature of the Zürau aphorisms, though they probably should not be interpreted exclusively according to the traditions of Jewish mysticism, for they represent primarily Kafka's *own* thoughts about the spiritual realities of human life. Kafka's meditations on "sin, suffering, hope and the true way" are profoundly spiritual and should not (and cannot) be expounded easily.[165] Their very nature forbids the schematizing or categorizing of their meaning.

To understand this meaning to some degree, one has to keep in mind the larger context of the Zürau aphorisms; they should be seen as an expression of Kafka's search for salvation. This search took him into the spiritual landscape of Hasidism, where he felt most at home, but he entered that landscape carrying all kinds of "western Jewish" luggage, including his personal "cares of the innermost existence." Among these cares was the realization that he had over the years become a compulsive self-observer (cf. T 221, 252, 282, 339, 462, 550). Now he came to feel that such self-observation was futile and harmful (although he never could free himself of the compulsive habit) (cf. T 552, 576). He raises the subject of self-observation and self-knowledge in the same notebooks that contain the aphorisms: "Wie kläglich ist meine Selbsterkenntnis, verglichen etwa mit meiner Kenntnis meines Zimmers. . . . Warum? Es gibt keine Beobachtung der innern Welt, so wie es eine der äußern gibt. . . . Die innere Welt läßt sich nur leben, nicht beschreiben" (H 72).

The "inner world" Kafka is talking about, cannot be described in terms of modern psychology: "Psychologie ist die Beschreibung der Spiegelung der irdischen Welt in der himmlischen Fläche oder richtiger: wie wir, Vollgesogene der Erde, sie uns denken, denn eine Spiegelung erfolgt gar nicht, nur wir sehen Erde, wohin wir uns auch wenden" (H 72). And in the sense that this "inner world" is not accessible through *description*, cannot be observed and analyzed, it is beyond language: "Die Sprache kann für alles außerhalb der sinnlichen Welt nur andeutungsweise, aber niemals auch nur annähernd vergleichsweise gebraucht werden, da sie, entsprechend der sinnlichen Welt, nur vom Besitz und seinen Beziehungen handelt" (H 92). The "inner world," the world of the soul, cannot be talked about in the same way the furniture of a room can be talked about. Whatever words are found to express this "inner world" merely seem to gesture vaguely in its direction, never capable of entering into it, touching only, as Kafka says, its surface (H 93). He concludes that the soul cannot know anything about itself, cannot, as it were, look at itself from the outside (H 93).

These remarks bring to mind the last sentence of Ludwig Wittgensteins's *Tractatus*: "Wovon man nicht sprechen kann, darüber muß man schweigen." According to this book, there are two areas of human experience that cannot be talked about meaningfully in the same way as the physical world: ethics and aesthetics. The language used by certain theological and aesthetic theorists to talk about religion and art seemed to Wittgenstein as improper as words seemed to Kafka when it came to describing the "inner world." Words, said Wittgenstein in his "Lecture on Ethics," "will only express facts; as a teacup will only hold a teacup full of water and if I were to pour a gallon over it" (WE 7). A book about ethics simply could not be written, and if it could, Wittgenstein says, it would "with an explosion destroy all the other books in the world" (WE 7).

Yet Wittgenstein considered the *Tractatus* a book about ethics, a book consisting of two parts, the written one and the unwritten, of which the second was by far the more important: "Es wird nämlich das Ethische durch mein Buch gleichsam von Innen her begrenzt; und ich bin überzeugt, daß es, *streng, nur* so zu begrenzen ist. Kurz, ich glaube: Alles was *viele* heute *schwefeln*, habe ich in meinem Buch festgelegt, indem ich darüber schweige" (WB 35).   He may have meant, as Paul Engelmann suggests, that by marking out the areas accessible to descriptive language he was defending the realm of ethics (and aesthetics) against an invasion by the nonsense of "natural," i.e., rationally constructed theology[166] and empirical psychology.[167]   However, as Rush Rhees and Cora Diamond have both pointed out, with the very attempt to identify what it is that can or cannot be said, one is already entering the realm of nonsense.[168]   Wittgenstein was aware of this paradoxical quality of his book, which is why, on its last page, he tells the reader that its sentences must be recognized as nonsense and be "thrown away like a ladder" on which one has climbed to a superior perspective. The reader has reached this vantage point when he understands not the sentences but their author.[169]   The sentences, in the sense that they are fundamentally nonsense, cannot be understood, but their author, as he expresses himself through the sentences, can.   For in the *Tractatus* Wittgenstein displays *why* one wants to talk about language in a certain (ultimately nonsensical) way, and understanding him can only consist in understanding *why* he wants to say the things he says in that book.

Even though his views about language changed considerably over the following years—he abandoned the search for the "general form of the proposition," for he came to think that such a search was based on confusion, and began to conceive of language as a complex network of language games, the "Mannigfaltigkeit der Sprachspiele" (WPI par. 23)[170]—he made the same point about understanding the author himself rather than his sentences at the end of his "Lecture on Ethics."   Wittgenstein gave this lecture almost ten years after he published the *Tractatus*.   It was to be a kind of "popular-scientific" (WE 4) explanation of the limitations of language with respect to art and religion. At its end Wittgenstein switches from talking about "people" running against the limits of language to speaking for himself. Later he made the following comment regarding this switch to Friedrich Waismann: "Hier läßt sich nichts mehr konstatieren, ich kann nur als Persönlichkeit hervortreten und in der ersten Person sprechen."[171]

Wittgenstein in his lecture had argued that whatever we say about ethics can only be said metaphorically (WE 7) or in similes: "For when we speak of God and that he sees everything and when we kneel and pray to him all our terms and actions seem to be parts of a great and elaborate allegory which represents him as a human being of great power whose grace we try to win, etc., etc." (WE 10). While this kind of allegory expresses certain human experiences which we would want to call religious, Wittgenstein says, the similes used (e.g., feeling "safe in the hands of God") cannot be paraphrased in ordinary language and therefore are not real similes. There are no facts "behind" them that could be described in "significant language" (WE 11), so that in the final analysis they are nothing but nonsense. Thus, even though the thoughts and feelings we want to express about ethics seem to Wittgenstein the most important thoughts and feelings in the world, seem to be of "absolute value," they simply cannot be put into "significant" words (WE 11). The metaphor used by the philosopher himself to describe the impossibility of writing a book about ethics illustrates his point. There are no facts behind the image of the exploding book which could be formulated in "significant language," yet Wittgenstein uses the picture to convey something about language and ethics that can be understood in some way in spite of its nonsensical character. But understanding in this case is very different from understanding a scientific description or a factual report, and to characterize this difference Wittgenstein described it as the one between understanding somebody's sentences and understanding the speaker himself. This shift of focus from someone's words to the person uttering those words has an important bearing on what Wittgenstein later was to call the grammar of religious language. I will return to it in connection with the discussion of some of the ways in which both Kafka and Wittgenstein conceived of that grammar.

If there can be no communication about ethics in "significant" language, any attempt to talk about it in such a language is bound to be pointless: "This running against the walls of our cage is perfectly, absolutely hopeless" (WE 12). The conclusion seems inescapable and final. And yet even at the time Wittgenstein wrote and gave his "Lecture on Ethics," he did not feel that the expression of religious thoughts and feelings was impossible, but rather that this kind of expression was fundamentally different from any factual statements and must not be treated as such. Instead of regarding religious utterances as basically nonsensical similes, he suggested in a conversation with Friedrich Waismann and Moritz Schlick, they should be considered a "Bestandteil der religiösen Handlung."[172] If a sentence like "I am safe in the hands of God" does not function in the same way as "significant" sentences, should not, for example, be looked at as essentially descriptive, then it must be accounted for differently. Regarding it as "part of religious activity" represents such an alternative understanding. My words appear the same as the words of ordinary language, but the similarity is only superficial, for when looked at more closely, they turn out to be more like, let's say, kneeling and folding my hands than reporting on my condition.

This explanation, however, still does not seem to do justice to the special character of my words, for it treats them too much like a kind of "simulated" language. In his conversation with Waismann, Wittgenstein said that for a sentence like "I feel safe in the hands of God" it really does not matter whether it is "true or false or nonsense." But that seems to be taking too much away from the sentence, for we *would* want to say that these things matter.[173]   Because Wittgenstein is still using "true, false and nonsense" in a sense close to the very special way he used them in his *Tractatus*, he is forced to, as it were, reclassify a certain form of human behavior previously described as language, as activity.   Activity might express meaning in some way, as kneeling does, but it cannot function like "true" language, cannot describe the facts of the world.   That Wittgenstein was tentatively reaching for this explanation, however, indicates in what direction his thoughts were taking him, for he eventually came to see language as closely connected with human activity.   And it also indicates his deep concern with the problem of the nature of religious language.

For Wittgenstein did not want to say that human beings were in principle cut off from verbally expressing their religious aspirations, but rather that the language used in the context of religion was in many ways remarkably different from the language used in, for example, science or history. This might explain why, in his conversations with Waismann and Schlick, he seems to have contradicted what he had said only shortly before in the "Lecture on Ethics": that we are hopelessly trapped in the "cage" of our language (WE 12). As Waismann reports, Wittgenstein made the this comment: "Anrennen gegen die Grenze der Sprache? Die Sprache ist ja kein Käfig."[174]   We would indeed be trapped as in a cage if we wanted to express religious experience in the language of science, describe the "inner world" as though it were a room; for such language would, as a matter of fact, be completely inadequate.

And this, as Wittgenstein was to say later in his *Philosophical Investigations*, would not simply be a matter of insufficient means, "als *könne* man etwas nicht": "Als wäre da wohl ein Gegenstand, von dem ich die Beschreibung abziehe, aber ich wäre nicht im Stande, ihn jemandem zu zeigen" (WPI par. 374). Rather, the kinds of things said and understood in the descriptive language of science cannot and do not play a meaningful role within the context of religious thought and activity. The information that praying in agriculture has been proven statistically ineffective, would not touch on what a farmer might be expressing with his prayer, nor would it in most cases be likely to make a difference in his actions or in his life. It belongs to the essence of religion, the later Wittgenstein would have said, that descriptive language does not play an important role in religious activities: "Das *Wesen* ist in der Grammatik ausgesprochen" (WPI par. 371). And we truly are cut off from the essence of religion (as though trapped in a cage) if we are blind to its grammar. (It was for this reason that Wittgenstein all his life abhorred theoretical theology.)

However, he would not have used the image of the cage to describe the language in which we express our religious experiences. Clearly, given the central role played by language in the relationship of human beings to the "world of the soul," Wittgenstein could not have meant to claim that a person submerged in prayer was really "running against the walls of a cage" or "running against the limits of language." While he was not sure how to think of the language of religion (or poetry), he did not direct the last sentence of the *Tractatus* against such language, only against the attempts of, for example, empirical psychology to talk about the "inner world" as though it were a room. In later years, Wittgenstein came to think the difference between the language of science and the language of religion could be described best as a difference in grammar, i.e., in terms of the role played by the words in their respective contexts. A remark from 1946 encapsulates his view with respect to religion: "Wie Du das Wort 'Gott' verwendest, zeigt nicht, *wen* Du meinst—sondern, was Du meinst" (WCV 50).

Rush Rhees, in his article on Wittgenstein's view of ethics, traces the development of that view from the *Tractatus* to the later works.[175]   That which is only implied by the *Tractatus* but not worked out there, is, as Rhees says, the significance of the conditions under which something is said.[176]   When and how words are said and also who is saying them are important in determining their meaning.   In the *Tractatus*, however, Wittgenstein was not interested in the surroundings of individual statements, but rather in what all statements had in common, their logical structure.[177]   He did not consider the context of the life and the activities to which ethical statements belonged, but only their apparent lack of such a logical structure.   This way of thinking about them must have been very disturbing for Wittgenstein, for according to his understanding the most meaningful sentences in prayer and poetry had to be excluded from "significant" language and thereby classified as nonsense.

His concern with this question shows itself in a letter he wrote to Paul Engelmann in 1917 (when he was still working on the manuscript of the *Tractatus*).   Here he gives an illustration of how "to express the inexpressible," and thus an early indication of his interest in what he might later have called the grammar of ethical and aesthetic language.[178] Engelmann had sent him Ludwig Uhland's poem "Graf Eberhards Weißdorn," and Wittgenstein comments on the way the poem successfully expresses the "inexpressible." The simple ballad tells about the life of a sincere and steadfast human being.   As a young man Graf Eberhard goes on a crusade to Palestine.   When he returns he brings with him a twig from a Palestinian hawthorn, which he plants and which grows over the years into a big tree.   In the last stanza, faintly reminiscent of Friedrich Müller's poem "Am Brunnen vor dem Tore," Graf Eberhard sits under his hawthorn tree dreaming of the old times and the faraway country. (Wittgenstein would have known "Am Brunnen vor dem Tore" for it had been set to music by Franz Schubert.) As in Müller's poem, the tree gently lures the sleeper into dreams and eventually, one may assume, into the deeper peace of death.   This poem seemed to Wittgenstein an excellent example of how the inexpressible could be expressed: "Das Uhlandsche Gedicht ist wirklich großartig. Und es ist so: Wenn man sich nicht bemüht das Unaussprechliche auszusprechen, so geht *nichts* verloren. Sondern das Unaussprechliche ist,—unaussprechlich—in dem Ausgesprochenen *enthalten!*"[179]

One may wonder how one is to conceive of the "inexpressible" in Uhland's poem and in what sense it might be contained in its words.   The poem, like a folk song, appears to move completely on the surface of events, without interpretation, evaluation or any metaphysical commentary. The events are held up to us like a series of pictures showing the successive stages of Graf Eberhard's life.   As they pass before us, they may give us a feeling for human life, the passage of time, our own lives, and many other things of this kind. In the count's pious and steadfast life, growing through the years just like the hawthorn tree, there seems to be no doubt or despair.   Count Eberhard, one might say, lives with what Wittgenstein describes in his "Lecture on Ethics" as the "experience of feeling *absolutely* safe" (WE 8).   This, among others, may have been an aspect of the poem that struck Wittgenstein as inexpressible, yet perfectly expressed.

Uhland's poem can thus be seen as making a profoundly ethical statement.   Even in his early thinking Wittgenstein allowed for the capability of language to express the unsayable.   Later he came to look on language in a different way and with this change of perspective his understanding of "expressing the inexpressible" also changed.   He no longer looked for the common logical structure of all "significant" sentences or thought that language was essentially descriptive, but rather began to focus on the "grammar" of language, i.e., when and under what conditions words were being used, for, as he once put it, "our words have meaning only in the stream of life" (WZ par. 135). It was this change of perspective that enabled him to resolve the problem of how to understand the kind of religious and poetic language his *Tractatus* perspective had forced him to declare nonsense. The problem itself may well have pointed him in this direction, for it guided his attention to the variety of ways in which language is used,[180] sometimes scientifically, sometimes descriptively, sometimes to comfort someone, sometimes to pray and so on.

In 1938, about nine years after he had given the "Lecture on Ethics," Wittgenstein in Cambridge gave a course on Belief. His lectures, preserved in the notes taken by his students, have been published under the title "Lectures on Religious Belief" (WA 53-72). At their beginning, he contrasts two hypothetical conversations: "Suppose someone were a believer and said: 'I believe in a Last Judgement,' and I said: 'Well, I'm not so sure. Possibly.' You would say that there is an enormous gulf between us. If he said: 'There is a German aeroplane overhead,' and I said 'Possibly, I'm not so sure,' you'd say we were fairly near" (WA 53). Talk about the Last Judgment takes place in a very different way from talk about aircraft, and much of what goes for one way, does not go for the other. One difference, for example, is that with respect to the aircraft we could point to all kinds of evidence to support our view, but with respect to the Last Judgment such evidence would be unlikely to influence us. In general, what we say is governed by entirely different rules: "My normal technique of language leaves me," says Wittgenstein (WA 55). And one way in which this difference comes out is that "you don't get in religious controversies, the form of controversy where one person is *sure* of the thing, and the other says: 'Well, possibly'" (WA 56).

In the days of the *Tractatus*, Wittgenstein tried to identify this difference in terms of "significant language" as opposed to the "nonsense" sentences used in religion and poetry. He later described the same difference as one of grammar. Kafka's aphorism about language, too, points toward the fact that the words and sentences we use in ordinary everyday life to describe, let's say, the furniture in our room, seem completely inappropriate when it comes to talking about the "inner world," the world of the soul. This world cannot be captured by such descriptive language, and if we insist on talking about it nevertheless, we can only do so "andeutungsweise," but never "vergleichsweise." An illustration of what Kafka might have meant is provided by a diary entry from January 16, 1922, in which he records his struggle to find the right words to describe his tormented state of mind (T 552 f.). He has experienced what he calls a "complete collapse," which he says can be taken in two ways, either as a lack of agreement between his "inner" and "outer clock" (the inner running wildly, the outer going along at a sluggish pace), or as a "Jagen . . . aus der Menschheit" (T 553). But "chase," he adds, is "only a picture" and he could just as well call it an "Ansturm gegen die letzte irdische Grenze" from "below," from the direction of humanity (T 553). This too, he concludes, is only a picture, and could be replaced by a third one, the picture of an assault "from above down toward me" (T 553).

There are no exact words that will capture his spiritual crisis. Or better: whatever words he finds, only seem to hint at this crisis, to intimate its character through pictures, without describing it "auch nur annähernd vergleichsweise." This, too, seems to be a characterization of the grammar of ethical language, for as Wittgenstein said in connection with the Uhland poem, the "inexpressible" is contained "inexpressibly" in the poet's words. Similarly, the pictures Kafka tentatively draws of his misery can be said to encapsulate that misery, without ever describing it in so many words. The pictures, as it were, have to speak for themselves, and whether they do depends not only on the artist who drew them but also on the response of their observer, his more or less spontaneous ability to "resonate" with them, as Wittgenstein once put it (WCV 58).   Such response is not a matter of any particular belief or opinion one may have formed, but rather depends on one's attitudes and dispositions—attitudes and dispositions that one shares, at least in some measure, with the artist and his culture. Wittgenstein, discussing the role of pictures played in religious language, says about our concept of the soul that it is not the expression of a belief, but that it involves a certain attitude toward other human beings: "Meine Einstellung zu ihm ist eine Einstellung zur Seele.   Ich habe nicht die *Meinung*, daß er eine Seele hat" (WPI par. 178).[181]   This is one of the ways in which language can communicate (more or less successfully) certain aspects of the "inner world."   Especially in the literature of religion there are many examples of extremely successful expressions of the "inexpressible," such as the parables of the New Testament, Zen poems or Hasidic anecdotes.   Such language "reaches" the world of the soul, or perhaps better, the soul of the listener, but it does so very differently from the way a description "reaches" the features of a room.

The following Hasidic anecdote is an illuminating example of this difference in grammar.   The Rabbi Schmelke and his brother asked their teacher, the Maggid of Mezeritz, to explain to them the words of the Mishnah: "A man must bless God for the evil in the same way that he blesses Him for the good which befalls."[182]   In his heart the Rabbi may have wondered why he was asked to assume, against all human reason and inclination, such an attitude toward his own suffering, and he may also have worried whether he could adopt it at all.   Instead of elucidating the troubling command, the Maggid sent the two to the Rabbi Sussya, who might explain it for them. At first Rabbi Sussya seemed to be the wrong person to ask questions about the proper attitude toward suffering, for, as he assured them laughingly, he himself had never "experienced anything but good all my days."[183]   However, since it was well-known that Rabbi Sussya's life was filled with the most "grievous sorrow," his words had an enlightening effect: "Thereupon they understood the meaning of the words of the Mishna, and the reason their Rabbi had sent them to the Rabbi Sussya."[184]

One way in which the language of religion might be characterized is by saying that it often talks through pictures. The way the anecdote makes its point is not through explanations formulated in discursive language, but rather by holding up the life of a human being who through his very actions shows how to understand the "words of the Mishna," embodies, as it were, its meaning.   It is the confrontation with this human being that brings about Rabbi Schmelke's sudden comprehension of the incomprehensible command. One is reminded here of Wittgenstein's insistence at the end of the *Tractatus* that the reader must understand its author rather than its sentences, and of his switch to the first person singular at the end of his "Lecture on Ethics."   For the ethical is communicated most perfectly through pictures, gestures, and, above all, through the attitudes and actions of human beings.

The pictures through which religion speaks do not by themselves clearly show how they are to be taken, as in the case of Rabbi Schmelke.   And it would not have helped him to recall situations of being grateful to a friend or a generous superior, for what makes sense in the context of everyday human relationships does not seem to make sense in that of religion.   Nor would any explanation psychology might be able to offer have helped the Rabbi, for the ways in which psychology looks at the world, the kinds of questions it asks and answers it gives, do not engage with the concerns and practices of religion. The mystifying pictures held up by religion can, as it were, only be understood in their application, only on the most personal level. Thus the command to thank God for one's misfortune might be described as a kind of picture, and Rabbi Sussya as its actual application. His life full of grief, borne with a smile as nothing "but good" from God, is what that picture means.

However, a person other than the Rabbi Schmelke might not have understood at all and gone away as confused as he had come, for Rabbi Sussya's presence was not bound to bring understanding, as, for example, the words: "This room faces south" in the appropriate context might be expected to do. Whether or not a picture will have an impact and provide insight, depends as much on the viewer's spiritual sensitivity and ability to respond as it does on this picture. The language of religion requires very different powers of comprehension from the language of factual reporting. Kafka, like Wittgenstein, was aware of this difference and concerned with the problem of how the "inner world" could be expressed and understood. His pictures seemed at times, as in his attempt to describe his tormented state of mind, inadequate and separated from the "real thing" as by a board. Yet at other times he must have felt that they expressed perfectly something that appeared to be inexpressible in any other way, as, for example, when he called "The Judgment" a poem (Br 148 f.). For the language of poetry, like that of religion, has to rely on pictures that, similar to gestures, can communicate in an instant and most poignantly something that a hundred words of discursive language cannot say. In this sense poetry and religious parables can be said to have an affinity to the language of gestures. The communicative power of gestures within the context of religion is illustrated by a Hasidic anecdote about a Rabbi who made people understand the meaning of prayer, not through any words of explanation, but through his *manner* of praying: "I heard that . . . when Rabbi Nahman sighed during prayer, he so broke the listener's heart that it seemed cut in two. The Besht said: 'Where Rabbi Nahman has visited, people know what prayer is; where Rabbi Nahman has not visited, people do not know what prayer is.'"[185]

How can such language, language that does not describe facts but rather tries to communicate the inexpressible through gestures, pictures and parables, be understood? This question is raised in Kafka's short prose text published by Brod under the title "Von den Gleichnissen" (E 328).[186] The first paragraph of the text is spoken by the representative of a group of people, who refers to himself and this group as "we." The problem with "the words of the sages," this speaker complains, is that they are merely parables and cannot be applied to daily life, which is "all we have." When the sage says "Go across" he means a "sagenhaftes Drüben" which he can't identify any more clearly, which therefore cannot "help us here at all," and which merely shows that the "incomprehensible is incomprehensible." Here, as in the Zürau aphorism about the limits of language, Kafka points to the difference in the way the "inner world" and one's room can be talked about, for the "words of the sages" concern that "inner world," but are "unverwendbar im täglichen Leben" and seem to have no relevance to its problems. The words used in everyday life, on the other hand, cannot describe the "mythological beyond," which therefore remains incomprehensible.

The second speaker, simply called "einer," appears to represent the side of the sages, for he points out how the parables are meant to be applied: "Würdet ihr den Gleichnissen folgen, dann wäret ihr selbst Gleichnisse geworden und damit schon der täglichen Mühe frei" (E 328). The implication of his words is the same as that of the story about Rabbi Schmelke's enlightening encounter with the Rabbi Sussya. The way to understand the parables of the sages is to live and act the way they suggest, for example, to strive to adopt Rabbi Sussya's attitude toward suffering, and in that sense *become* the parables. Such understanding is not a matter of intellectual comprehension expressible in discursive language, but rather a matter of, as Wittgenstein puts it in a similar context, changing one's life (WCV 27).

Wittgenstein seems to anticipate an objection the first speaker in Kafka's meta-parable might well voice, the objection that someone like Rabbi Sussya is simply living like a "mole," blind to the problem of life, and the philosopher answers it with the following suggestion: "Oder soll ich nicht sagen: daß, wer richtig lebt, das Problem nicht als *Traurigkeit*, also doch nicht problematisch, empfindet, sondern vielmehr als eine Freude; also gleichsam als einen lichten Äther um sein Leben, nicht als einen fraglichen Hintergrund" (WCV 27). But the difficulty with Kafka's parables and Wittgenstein's metaphor of "lichter Äther" is that in the final analysis whether or not we understand them depends on us, our own ability to "catch on," and in that sense is not guaranteed by the words.

This is illustrated by the dialogue that ends Kafka's story. The first speaker's reaction to the invitation to "follow" and thereby "become" the parables, shows that the point has eluded him. Switching from "we" to "I," he objects: "Ich wette, daß auch das ein Gleichnis ist" (E 328). In other words he has chosen to remain outside the parable, and while he is correct in assuming that the words of the second speaker can only be understood in the way all parables are understood, he has lost out in terms of the parable, for, failing to "catch on," he has to continue carrying his burden of "tägliche Mühen" as before. Wittgenstein, as concerned with the problem of understanding religious parables as Kafka, comments on the danger of taking such stories in a way they are not meant to be taken and thereby missing their point. Religious similes, he says, move "on the edge of the abyss" in that they invite the wrong interpretation if they are given the shape of an argument from which one is to draw certain logical conclusions, such as that God should be loved *because* He is generous.

Thus, the spiritual advice to thank God for the good one has received, but not to complain about one's suffering, would be easier to accept, Wittgenstein says, if it were made clear that our relationship to God is not at all like that to other people, whose alternate generosity and abuse we would naturally resent. Similarly, the invitation to thank the bees for their honey "as though they were good people" seems appropriate to Wittgenstein, but not to be told to thank them *because* they are good, for "the next moment they may sting you" (WCV 29). Parables have to be taken in a certain way, or else they will be misunderstood: "Es werden Lebensregeln in Bilder gekleidet. Und diese Bilder können nur dienen, zu *beschreiben*, was wir tun sollen, aber nicht dazu, es zu *begründen*. Denn um zu begründen, müßten sie auch weiter stimmen. . . . Die Religion sagt: *Tu dies!—Denk so!*—aber sie kann es nicht begründen, und versucht sie es auch nur, so stößt sie ab; denn zu jedem Grund, den sie gibt, gibt es einen stichhaltigen Gegengrund. Überzeugender ist es, zu sagen: 'Denke so!—so seltsam dies scheinen mag.' Oder: 'Möchtest Du das nicht tun?—so abstoßend es ist'" (WCV 29).

In one of his first letters to Milena Jesenská, Kafka made a very similar remark that throws a great deal of light on his much-discussed parable. He says about Christ: "Er konnte nur sagen: 'Folge mir nach' und dann dieses große (das ich leider ganz falsch citiere): tue nach meinem Wort und du wirst sehn, daß es nicht das Wort eines Menschen, sondern Gottes Wort ist" (M 25). So this is a further way in which the grammar of religious language could be described. Causal explanations and concepts of utility or profit have no room in it. And it is precisely this point that Kafka's meta-parable wants to make. For when the first speaker complains that the words of the sages are "inapplicable in daily life," and that no profitable results can be expected from following them, he is making the grammatical mistake of talking about the soul as though it were a room.

One year before he died, Kafka spent about a month in Müritz, a seaside resort on the Baltic, where he met Dora Dymant, the nineteen-year-old daughter of Hasidic Jews from Poland, who was running the kitchen of a vacation home for Jewish children at Müritz.[187] Kafka eventually decided to live with her in Berlin, and it may well be that the months she shared his life were his happiest. A few days after he met her, he sent a post card to his friend Robert Klopstock, on which he makes an observation that seems to hint at the grammar of religious and poetic language and could well serve as a general motto for the writer Kafka: "Mitteilbares habe ich eigentlich nichts, zu Zeigendes viel, Mit-zu-Erlebendes viel" (Br 438).

Conclusion

The purpose of this study, taking to heart Wittgenstein's insistence on attention to individual cases, has been to explore in some detail Kafka's relationship to language. This relationship, as has emerged from the discussion of its various aspects, was highly complex and cannot simply be labeled as one of "skepticism" or be understood as another example of the "radikale Sprachkritik" that was characteristic of the "Sprachkrise" occurring in central Europe around the turn of this century.[188] Kafka certainly did not consider language as a "leeres Getriebensein"[189] or hold the view that "language superficially and conventionally applies to the world, but the thing itself cannot be said to correspond to anything or constitute anything that could meaningfully be called truth."[190] Most of the problems he encountered in relation to language arose from the conditions of his life and not from theoretical considerations of this kind.

Kafka himself, his specific environment and his personal attitudes have been explored by this study. Any human being growing up the way he did might be left with certain worries about language. German, Kafka's native language, in important ways was not his "language from the heart," and it seemed there was no other language that could be. The misfortune of not having a language of one's own was crystallized for him (as for Mauthner) in the fact that he did not possess a dialect. It represented an important aspect of the way he saw himself, that is, as a typical "western Jew" who had no roots anywhere, neither in the traditional Jewish culture left behind, nor in the German culture whose traditions appeared to him curiously inaccessible.

In his relations with other people, language often failed to serve Kafka as a medium for contact. That he suffered from his inability to communicate easily with others emerges from his diaries. What appeared to many who met him as polite reticence reveals itself in the diaries as painful feelings of human inadequacy and isolation. And just as for Kafka the lack of a dialect became symbolic of his cultural alienation, the fact that he could not engage with others in comfortable conversation became symbolic of his failure to prove himself as a worthy member of the human race. One important aspect of his relationship to language, then, is the way language contributed to his sense of cultural and human alienation.

These negative aspects, however, should not make us overlook his intense love of language, which represented, after all, the medium of his art, the fuel that powered his "dream capsule" on its night rides.[191] When he considered language, which he often did, he conceived of it in a great variety of vivid images and metaphors, for here, as everywhere in his work, he instinctively preferred to express himself in pictures. Closely related to this preference was his fascination for gestures and mannerisms, expressing itself in his writing as well as in his passion for reading aloud and in his admiration for the fiery Yiddish performances of his friend Löwy. Brod may well have been blind to much in Kafka, and yet his insistence on his friend's capability for the "joy of life" points to a side of Kafka's that tends to be overlooked and that should be taken into account, especially in a study of his relationship to language.

For Kafka derived a great deal of pleasure from language, delighted in it, played with it, excelled in it, marveled at its manifestations in human life. He may at times have felt frustrated with language, especially when the writing was going badly, but he tended to blame himself rather than language for his difficulties, himself and "the office" which kept him away from writing. And he also experienced moments of intoxicating pleasure, when language poured out of him in marvelous sentences, so that it would be very misleading to draw him as a writer who looked on his medium with fundamental distrust. He was struck by language as a living phenomenon, a manifestation of the human spirit and an integral part of human life; it is hard to fit all this into the one-dimensional perspective of theoretical skepticism Kafka is sometimes said to have adopted.

When he sought to formulate his thoughts on religion, he felt that he had encountered the true limits of language, and he described these limits by pointing out that the "inner world" of the soul cannot be described in the way a room can. Communication about this "inner world" seemed to Kafka very different from communication about furniture. It is this difference that his meta-parable "Von den Gleichnissen" brings out by emphasizing the fact that understanding its meaning is primarily a matter of being able to respond in a certain way. Kafka's insights into the language of religion have a remarkable affinity with those of Wittgenstein. They also bear in an important way on his understanding of language as his artistic medium. For he conceived of both the language of religion and the language of his art as relying largely on pictures and gestures to convey meaning, and as depending for their comprehension on the listener's ability to respond. Even when he came to define the limits of descriptive language with respect to the "inner world," Kafka can thus hardly be said to have adopted a skeptical stance.

Notes

1. For a good description of these conditions representing them in their larger historical context, cf. *Ernst Pawel, The Nightmare of Reason: A Life of Franz Kafka* (New York: Random House, 1984), pp. 3-16.

2. Thomas Mann, *Ausgewählte Erzählungen* (Stockholm: Bermann-Fischer Verlag, 1948), p.123.

3. Ibid., p.157.

4. Cf. also Pavel Eisner, *Franz Kafka and Prague* (New York: Golden Griffin Books, 1950), p. 26; Peter Demetz,"Noch einmal: Prager Deutsch," *Literatur und Kritik*, 6 (1966), 58-59; Emil Skala,"Das Prager Deutsch," *Zeitschrift für deutsche Sprache*, 22 (1966), 84-91; Ritchie Robertson, *Kafka: Judaism, Politics and Literature* (Oxford: Clarendon Press, 1985), p.2.

5. Egon Kisch, *Die Abenteuer in Prag* (Wien, Prag, Leipzig: Verlag Ed. Strache, 1920), pp.276-285. Also: Pavel Trost "Das späte Prager Deutsch," *Germanistica Pragensia*, 2 (1962) 31-39; Heinz Politzer, "Zur Kafka-Philologie," *Franz Kafka*, ed. H. Politzer, Wege der Forschung 322

(Darmstadt: Wissenschaftliche Buchgesellschaft, 1973), 159-161; Felix Weltsch, "The Rise and Fall of the Jewish-German Symbiosis—the Case of Franz Kafka," *Leo Baeck Institute Yearbook*, 1 (1959), 255-276, 258; Pawel, op. cit., p.30 ff; 38; for further sources: Richard Thieberger, "Sprache," *Kafka-Handbuch*, ed. Hartmut Binder, 2 vols., (Stuttgart: Alfred Kröner Verlag, 1979), II, 177-203.

6. Cf. for a more scientific account and further sources, Pavel Trost, op. cit., 35.

7. Ibid.

8. Ibid., 31.

9. Cf. also Susanne Kessler, *Kafka—Poetik der sinnlichen Welt* (Stuttgart: J.B. Metzlersche Verlagsbuchhandlung, 1983), pp.9, 13, 24, 36.

10. Cf. Marlis Gerhard *Die Sprache Kafkas. Eine semiotische Untersuchung*, diss. Stuttgart, 1969, pp.73-81.

11. Cf. also Hans Tramer, "Prague—City of Three Peoples,"*Leo Baeck Institute YB*, 9 (1964), 305-39; Pawel, op. cit., 30 ff., 136.

12. For the Prague school system, cf. Pawel, op. cit., pp.23,24,33,47,59,73.

13. Kisch, Egon. *Vom Marktplatz der Sensationen* (London: Verlag Jugend Voran, 1943; new ed. Berlin: Aufbau Verlag, 1949), p.85; cf. also Eisner, op. cit., p.23 ff.

14. Ibid.

15. Cf. also Eisner, op. cit., p.26; Robertson, op. cit., p.2.

16. For discussions of Kafka and Prague, cf. Heinz Politzer, "Prague and the Origins of Rainer Maria Rilke, Franz Kafka, and Franz Werfel," *Modern Language Quarterly,* 16 (1955), 49-62; Willy Haas, "Geheimnisse des alten Prag," W.H., *Die literarische Welt* (München: Paul List Verlag, 1957), pp.9-39, esp. pp.30-39; H.Politzer, "Dieses Mütterchen hat Krallen," *Literatur und Kritik,* 9 (1974), 15-33; Christoph Stölzl, *Kafkas böses Böhmen. Zur Sozialgeschichte eines Prager Juden* (München: text und kritik GmbH, 1975); Julius M. Herz, "Franz Kafka and Austria: National Background and Ethnic Identity," *Modern Austrian Literature* 11 no. 3/4 (1978), 301-318; Hartmut Binder, *Kafka. Ein Leben in Prag* (München: Mahnert-Lueg, 1982); Leonhard Brosch, *Kafka und Prag* (Pfullingen: Verlag Günther Neske, 1983); Jiří Gruša, *Franz Kafka of Prague,* tr. Eric Mosbacher (New York: Schocken Books, 1983); Hans-Gerd Koch, "Chronik zum jungen Kafka im Umkreis des kulturellen Lebens von Prag," *Der junge Kafka,* ed. Gerhard Kurz (Frankfurt/M: Suhrkamp, 1984), pp.242-252.

17. Weltsch, op. cit., 258.

18. Thieberger, op. cit., 177.

19. Trost, op. cit., 38.

20. Eisner, op. cit., p.97.

21. Cf. also Eisner, op. cit., p.19; Heinz Politzer, 1955, 49-62, 52.

22. Fritz Mauthner, *Prager Jugendjahre* (Frankfurt/M: S.Fischer Verlag, 1969), p. 30.

23. Cf. Joachim Kühn, *Gescheiterte Sprachkritik* (Berlin, New York: Walter de Gruyter, 1975), pp.142-174, esp. 173; for further literature on Mauthner, cf. Elisabeth Leinfellner, "Zur nominalistischen Begründung von Linguistik und Sprachphilosophie: Fritz Mauthner und Ludwig Wittgenstein," *Studium Generale*, 22 (1969), 209-251; Gershon Weiler, *Mauthner's Critique of Language* (Cambridge: University Press, 1970); Walter Eschenbacher, *Fritz Mauthner und die deutsche Literatur um 1900* (Frankfurt/M: Peter Lang, 1977); Martin Stern, "Der Briefwechsel Hofmannsthal—Fritz Mauthner," *Hofmannsthal Blätter*, (1978), H 19/20, 21-39; Linda Ben-Zvi, "Samuel Beckett, Fritz Mauthner, and the Limits of Language," *PMLA*, 95 (1980), 183-200.

24. Mauthner, op. cit., p.49.

25. Ibid.

26. I am using this expression in reference to Brod's book, not the famous Linguistic Circle of Prague.

27. Kurt Tucholsky, *Ausgewählte Briefe* (Hamburg: Rowohlt Verlag, 1960), p.473; cf. Thieberger, op. cit., 178.

28. Cf. Anthony Thorlby, "Kafka and Language," *The World of Franz Kafka*, ed. J.P. Stern (New York: Holt, Rinehart and Winston, 1980), pp.133-144; Susanne Kessler, op. cit.; Wolf Kittler, *Der Turmbau zu Babel und das Schweigen der Sirenen. Über das Reden, das Schweigen, die Stimme und die Schrift in vier Texten von Franz Kafka* (Erlangen: Verlag Palme & Enke, 1985); Detlef Kremer, *Die Erotik des Schreibens* (Frankfurt/M: Athenäum, 1989), p. 66 f.

29. As Hans Dieter Zimmermann has already pointed out, Kafka was not a language skeptic in the style of Mauthner. However, Zimmermann fails to see the affinity of Kafka's and Ludwig Wittgenstein's perception of language, primarily because Zimmermann regards Wittgenstein as such a skeptic. H.D.Z., "Franz Kafka und das Judentum," *Juden und Judentum in der Literatur*, ed. Herbert A. Strauss und Christhard Hoffmann (München: Deutscher Taschenbuch Verlag, 1985), pp.237-253, p.250.

30. *Die Fruchtschale, Chinesische Lyrik vom 12. Jahrhundert vor Chr. bis zur Gegenwart*, tr. and ed. Hans Heilmann (München & Leipzig: R. Piper & Co., 1905).

31. Heilmann, op. cit., pp.56 f.

32. Eisner, op. cit., p.8.

33. Cf. Politzer 1955, 56.

34. Wilhelm Busch, *Historisch-kritische Gesamtausgabe*, ed. Friedrich Bohne, 4 vols. (Zürich: Stauffacher Verlag, 1959), IV, 449-515, 469.

35. Cf. e.g., Tucholsky, op. cit., p.473; for further recollections of personal encounters with Kafka, cf. Ludwig Hardt, "Erinnerung an Franz Kafka," *Neue Rundschau*, 58 (1947), 239-242; Max Brod, "Keine Flickarbeit. Eine Erinnerung an Franz Kafka anläßlich seines fünfundzwanzigsten Todestages im Juni 1949," *Berliner Hefte*, 4 (1949), 7-9; J.P. Hodin, "Erinnerungen an Franz Kafka," *Der Monat*, 1 (1949), 89-96, containing the recollections of the painter F. Feigl and Dora Dymant; Johannes Urzidil, "Begegnungen mit Franz Kafka," *Neue Literarische Welt*, No.2 (Jan.25, 1952), 3; Marthe Robert,

"Dora Dymants Erinnerungen an Kafka," *Merkur*, 7 (1953), 848-851; Friedrich Thieberger, "Erinnerungen an Franz Kafka," *Eckart*, 23 (1953/54) 49-53, which I was unable to look at, but would like to include for the sake of completeness; J. Urzidil, "Edison und Kafka," *Der Monat*, 13 (1960/61), 53-57; M.Brod, "Aus Kafkas Freundeskreis," *Wort in der Zeit*, 10 (1964), 4-6; Willy Haas, "Das Unvergessene," *Wort in der Zeit*, 10 (1964), 8-10; Samuel Hugo Bergmann, "Erinnerungen an Franz Kafka," *Universitas*, 27 (1972), 739-50, which I was also unable to look at; Gertrude Urzidil, "My Personal Meetings with Franz Kafka," *Journal of Modern Literature*, 6 (1977), 446-447.

36. For the business of Kafka's father, cf. Wagenbach, *Franz Kafka in Selbstzeugnissen und Bilddokumenten* (Hamburg: Rowohlt Taschenbuch Verlag, 1964), p.16.

37. Cf. *Fragmente, Herders sämtliche Werke*, ed. Bernhard Suphan, 33 vols. (Berlin: Weidmann, 1877-1913), I, 151 ff.

38. Cf. e.g., Jacob Grimm, *Über den Ursprung der Sprache* (Berlin: Ferdinand Dümmler's Verlagsbuchhandlung, 1858), pp. 12 f.; Wilhelm von Humboldt, "Allgemeine Betrachtung des menschlichen Entwicklungganges," *Über die Verschiedenheit des menschlichen Sprachbaues, Werke in fünf Bänden*, ed. Andreas Flitner and Klaus Giel (Stuttgart: J.G. Cotta'sche Buchhandlung, 1963), III, 384-392. For a discussion of Herder's perspective and its affinity with Humboldt's thought as well as that of more recent writers, among them Karl Kraus, cf. James W. Marchand, "Herder: Precursor of Humboldt, Whorf and Modern Language Philosophy," *Johann Gottfried Herder: Innovator Through the Ages*, ed. Wulf Koepke in cooperation with Samson B. Knoll, Modern German Series, 10, (Bonn: Bouvier, 1982), 20-34.

Wittgenstein, too, belongs to this school of thought. Cf. Rüdiger Böhle, "Der Begriff der Sprache bei Wilhelm von Humboldt und Ludwig Wittgenstein," *Dimensionen der Sprache in der Philosophie des deutschen Idealismus, Bruno Liebrucks zum 70. Geburtstag zugeeignet*, ed. Brigitte Scheer und Günter Wohlfahrt (Würzburg: Königshausen & Neumann, 1982), pp.190-213.

39. Cf. Mechthild Borries, *Ein Angriff auf Heinrich Heine. Kritische Betrachtungen zu Karl Kraus*, Studien zur Poetik und Geschichte der Literatur 13 (Stuttgart, Berlin, Köln, Mainz: Verlag W. Kohlhammer, 1971), 43 ff.

40. Cf. Borries, op. cit., 44.

41. For a detailed account of Kafka's involvement with the Yiddish theater, cf. H. Binder, *Kafka-Kommentar zu den Romanen, Rezensionen, Aphorismen und zum Brief an den Vater* (München: Winkler Verlag, 1976), pp.387-403. As Robertson mentions, Isaac Bashevis Singer has portrayed Löwy as "Jacques Kohn" in the story "A Friend of Kafka" (I.B.Singer, *A Friend of Kafka and Other Stories* (New York: Farrar, Straus & Giroux, 1970), pp. 3-16); for Löwy's fate cf. also: Lucy Dawidowicz, *The War against the Jews* (London: Weidenfeld and Nicolson, 1975), p.257; cf., Robertson, op. cit., p.28.

42. Cf. Mauthner, op. cit., pp.30-31.

43. Cf. M.Pinès, *Histoire de la littérature judéo-allemande* (Paris: Jouve et Cie, 1911), p.87 ff.; for a short biography of Pinès, cf. Robertson, op. cit., p.18.

44. Cf. N. Susskind, "How Yiddish Originated," *Judah A. Joffe Book*, ed. Yudel Mark (New York: Yivo Institute for

Jewish Research, 1958), pp.146-157; *Encyclopaedia Judaica* (Jerusalem, Israel: Keter Publishing House Ltd., 1971), XVI, col.789-798; Israel Zinberg, *A History of Jewish Literature*, tr. and ed. Bernhard Martin, 12 vols. (New York: KTAV Publishing House, Inc., 1972-78), VII, 3-28; Max Weinreich, *History of the Yiddish Language* (Chicago and London: University of Chicago Press, 1973), pp.328-347, pp.719-173; J.W. Marchand, "Proto Yiddish and the Glosses: Can We Reconstruct Proto Yiddish?," *Origins of the Yiddish Language*, Winter Studies in Yiddish, vol I, Papers from the First Annual Oxford Winter Symposium in Yiddish Language and Literature, 15-17 December 1985, ed. Dovid Katz (Oxford: Pergamon Press, 1987), 83-94.

45. Cf. Marchand, op. cit.; N. Susskind, "A Partisan History of Yiddish," *Origins of the Yiddish Language*, 127-134; H. Graetz, *Volkstümliche Geschichte der Juden*, 3 vols. (Leipzig: O. Leiner 1888-89), rept. Berlin, Wien: Benjamin Harz Verlag, 1922), II, 181-202.

46. Cf. Max Weinreich, "Outlines of Western Yiddish," *Juda A. Joffe Book*, ed. Yudel Mark, New York: Yivo Institute for Jewish Research, 1958, pp.158-194.

47. Cf. also Hans Tramer, op. cit., 305; Chris Bezzel, *Kafka Chronik*, Reihe Hanser 178 (München-Wien: Hanser Verlag, 1975), 7; Robertson, op. cit., p.2.

48. Cf. Evelyn Torton Beck, *Kafka and the Yiddish Theater: Its Impact on His Work* (Madison, Milwaukee and London: The University of Wisconsin Press, 1971), p.227.

49. Cf. Leo Wiener, *The History of Yiddish Literature in the Nineteenth Century* (London: John C. Nimmo, 1899), p.215; Meyer Waxman, *A History of Jewish Literature from*

the Close of the Bible to Our Own Days, 4 vols. (New York: Bloch Publishing Co., 1936), IV, 463-545, esp. 469 and 489; A.A. Roback, "Birth of Literary Criticism," *The Story of Yiddish Literature* (New York: Yiddish Scientific Institute, 1940), pp.245-257; Sol Liptzin, "Yiddish Ideologies," S.L., *A History of Yiddish Literature* (Middle Village, N.Y.: Jonathan David Publishers, 1972), pp.112-135.

50. Cf. M.Pinès, pp.31-54; Waxman, op. cit., IV, 463-544.

51. Cf. J.G. Herder "Auszug aus einem Briefwechsel über Ossian und die Lieder der alten Völker," op. cit., V, 159-207.

52. For the development of Yiddish literature, cf. Waxman, op. cit., ibid.; *Enc. Judaica*, XVI, col.798-833.; Israel Zinberg, op. cit., VII, 29-48.

53. Cf. Liptzin *Flowering of Yiddish Literature* (New York, London: Thomas Yoseloff, 1963), pp.101, 115, 117 f.; the same, 1972, pp. 64 ff.; it is interesting in this context, although not directly related to the issue of rehabilitation of the Yiddish language, that Goethe was quite struck by the expressive quality of Yiddish and spoke it well. Cf. J.W. Marchand, "Goethes 'Judenpredigt'," *Monatshefte*, 50 (1958), 305-310.

54. For the origins of the Yiddish theater, cf. *Enc. Judaica*, XV, col.1064-1092; Nahma Sandrow, *Vagabond Stars: A World History of Yiddish Theater* (New York: Seth Press, 1977), pp.1-39, for its development in the nineteenth and twentieth century, ibid., pp. 40-411.

55. Beck, op. cit., p.226.

56. Kafka owned the 1923 edition (Berlin, Wien: Benjamin Harz Verlag), cf. Wagenbach, 1958, p.256.

57. Graetz, op. cit., III, 473.

58. As Robertson points out, the notes Kafka took from Graetz' book do not appear in the German edition of his diaries, but are included in their English translation by Joseph Kresh. Cf. *The Diaries of Franz Kafka*, 2 vols. (New York: Schocken Books, 1948), I, 224-7; Robertson, op. cit., p.19.

59. Cf. Jacob Gerzon, *Die jüdisch-deutsche Sprache: Eine grammatikalisch-lexikalische Untersuchung ihres deutschen Grundbestandes* (Frankfurt/M: J. Kauffmann, 1902); S.A. Birnbaum, *Yiddish: A Survey and a Grammar* (Toronto, Buffalo: University of Toronto Press 1979), pp.197-307; Uriel Weinreich, *College Yiddish: An Intro-duction to the Yiddish Language and to Jewish Life and Culture* (New York: Yiddish Scientific Institute—Yivo, sec-ond revised edition, 1953); for further sources, cf. Uriel and Beatrice Weinreich, *Yiddish Language and Folklore: A Selective Bibliography for Research* (S'-Gravenhage: Mouton & Co., 1959).

60. For a discussion of how much standardization of a language is needed before literary forms can develop in that language, cf. Bohuslav Havránek, "The Functional Differen-tiation of the Standard Language," *A Prague School Reader on Aesthetics, Literary Structure, and Style*, ed. and tr. from the original Czech by Paul L. Garvin (Washington, D.C.: Georgetown University Press, 1964), pp.3-16; Jan Muka-řovský, "Standard Language and Poetic Language," ibid., pp.17-30.

61. Cf. Beck, op. cit. pp.12-30.

62. Cf. Pinès, op. cit., p.115.

63. Cf. ibid.

64. Cf. also Robertson, op. cit., p.18.

65. Cf. Pinès, op. cit., pp.8-9.

66. Cf. also Pawel, op. cit., p.18

67. Cf. Weltsch, op. cit., 267.

68. For the secondary literature on this work, cf. H. Binder, 1975, p.230; Gerhard Neumann, "Die Arbeit im Alchimistengäßchen," *Kafka-Handbuch*, II, 313-349, 342; for a detailed discussion of the rather large body of literature on Kafka's little story, cf. Günter Saße, "Die Sorge des Lesers. Zu Kafkas Erzählung 'Die Sorge des Hausvaters'," *Poetica*, 10 (1978), 262-284; especially noteworthy is Walter Höllerer's "Odradek unter der Stiege." Eröffnungsreferat für das Franz-Kafka-Symposium London, 20.10. 1983, *Sprache im technischen Zeitalter* (1983), 350-362.

69. Cf. Gerd Backenköhler, "Neues zum 'Sorgenkind Odradek'," *ZDP*, 89 (1970), 269-273, 273.

70. Graetz, op. cit., III, 470.

71. Cf. Bezzel, op. cit., 193 ff.

72. Kessler, op. cit., pp 10-23.

73. Cf. also Ernst Pawel, "Kafkas Judentum," *Kafka und das Judentum*, ed. Karl Erich Grözer, Stéphan Mosès, Hans Dieter Zimmermann (Frankfurt/M: Jüdischer Verlag bei Athenäum, 1987), pp. 253-258, p.255.

74. Weltsch, op. cit., 267.

75. Cf. also Gerhard Kurz, "Schnörkel und Schleier und Warzen. Die Briefe Kafkas an Oskar Pollak und seine literarischen Anfänge," *Der junge Kafka*, ed. Gerhard Kurz (Frankfurt/M: Suhrkamp, 1984), pp.68-101, pp.71 f.

76. Cf. Graetz, op. cit., III, 469 ff., Waxman, op. cit., III, 18-84, esp. 63-77; Wilfried Barner, "Vorurteil, Empirie, Rettung. Der junge Lessing und die Juden," *Juden und Judentum in der Literatur*, ed. Herbert A. Strauss and Christhard Hoffmann, (München: Deutscher Taschenbuch Verlag, 1985), pp.52-77.

77. Cf. Alexander Altmann, *Moses Mendelssohn: A Biographical Study* (University: University of Alabama Press, 1973), pp.37-8.

78. Cf. Altmann, op. cit., pp.39-40.

79. Waxman, op. cit., III, 65; cf. also: Altmann, op. cit., pp.112-129, esp. pp.116-118.

80. Cf. Altmann, op. cit., pp.370 ff.

81. Ibid.

82. Ibid., p.378.

83. Cf. Jeffrey L. Sammons, *Heinrich Heine: A Modern Biography* (Princeton, N.J.: Princeton University Press, 1979), pp.15 f.

84. Moses Mendelssohn, *Gesammelte Schriften*, ed. I.Elbogen, Alexander Altmann, 19 vols. (Stuttgart, Bad Cannstadt: Friedrich Frommann Verlag, 1971-74), VII, 279,

for Mendelssohn's role as political reformer, cf. Altmann, op. cit., pp.421-552.

85. Cf. Eric Blackall, *The Emergence of German as a Literary Language* (Cambridge: University Press, 1959), pp. 351-371; Hans Eggers, *Deutsche Sprachgeschichte*, 2 vols. (Hamburg: Rowohlts Enzyklopädie, 1986), II, 323-352.

86. Weltsch, op. cit., 264; cf. also Brod, *Prager Kreis*, pp.40 ff.

87. Cf. Altmann, op. cit., pp. 569 ff.

88. Cf. Graetz, op. cit., III, 471.

89. Cf. Altmann, op. cit., p.39.

90. Cf. Jeffrey Sammons, op. cit., pp.37-38; Ruth L. Jacobi, *Heines jüdisches Erbe* (Bonn: Bouvier Verlag Herbert Grundmann, 1978), pp.40-48; S.S. Prawer, *Heine's Jewish Comedy* (Oxford: Clarendon Press, 1983), pp.7 ff; Brod, 1966, p.40; Hartmut Kircher, *Heinrich Heine und das Judentum* (Bonn: Bouvier Verlag Herbert Grundmann, 1973), pp.93-100.

91. Cf. Waxman, op. cit., IV, 568-576.

92. Cf. Gabriele Cooper, "Tanzende Chiffren: Heines Faust," *Maske und Kothurn*, 12 (1986) 41-52.

93. Cf. Mechthild Borries, op. cit., 28.

94. Cf. ibid., 18 ff.

95. Cf. Friedrich Jenaczek, *Zeittafeln zur "Fackel".* *Themen, Ziele, Probleme* (München: Kösel Verlag, 1965), pp.1-109.

96. Cf. Leo Berg, "Detlev von Liliencron und die moderne Lyrik," *Das Magazin für Literatur,* 69 (1900), Nr.50, col.1241-1244 and Nr. 51, col.1269, rept. *Literarische Manifeste der Jahrhundertwende. 1890-1910,* ed. Erich Ruprecht & Dieter Bänsch (Stuttgart: J.B. Metzlersche Verlagsbuchhandlung, 1970), pp.72-76. For the concepts of sincerity and immediacy in literature, cf. Patricia Ball, "Sincerity: The Rise and Fall of a Critical Term," *MLR,* 19, 1964, 1-11; Lionel Trilling, *Sincerity and Authenticity* (Cambridge, Mass.: Harvard University Press, 1972); Wallace Jackson, *Immediacy: The Development of a Critical Concept from Addison to Coleridge,* Amsterdam: Rodopi, 1973). For a discussion of the related issue of authenticity in art, cf. Dagmar Barnouw, "Loos, Kraus, Wittgenstein and the Problem of Authenticity," *The Turn of the Century: German Literature and Art 1890-1915,* ed. Gerald Chapple and Hans H. Schulte, The McMaster Colloquium on German Literature (Bonn: Bouvier Verlag, 1981), pp.249-273.

97. Hans Benzmann, "Die Entwicklung der modernen deutschen Lyrik," *Moderne deutsche Lyrik,* ed. H.B. (Leipzig: P. Reclam jun., 1924), pp.5-56, p.14.

98. Julius Hart, "Die Entwicklung der neueren Lyrik in Deutschland," *Pan,* 4 (1896), Nr.1, pp.33-40, rept. *Literarische Manifeste,* pp.5-23, p.10. For Liliencron's reception by contemporaries cf. also: Fritz Böckel, *Detlev von Liliencron. Erinnerungen und Urteile,* 2nd., enlarged ed. of *Liliencron im Urteil zeitgenössischer Dichter* (Leipzig: Xenien-Verlag, 1912).

99. Cf. Heinrich Spiero, *Detlev von Liliencron. Sein Leben und seine Werke* (Berlin & Leipzig: Schuster & Loeffler, 1913).

100. Cf. Ute Schaub, "Liliencron und Heine im Urteil von Karl Kraus," *Heine Jahrbuch*, 18 (1979), 191-201.

101. Cf. also Borries, op. cit., 25.

102. Cf. Schaub, op. cit., p.192; Detlev von Liliencron, *Gesammelte Werke*, ed. Richard Dehmel, 8 vols. (Berlin: Schuster & Loeffler, 1911), III, 109.

103. Cf. Borries, op. cit., 25.

104. Cf. Gerald Stieg "Kafka als Spiegel der Kraus'schen Literaturpolemik," *Kontroversen, alte und neue*, ed. Franz Josef Worstbrock (Tübingen: Niemeyer, 1986), pp.98-106.

105. Cf. also Bezzel, op. cit., 25.

106. Cf. Sammons, op. cit., pp.14-15.

107. Alfred Meißner, *Geschichte meines Lebens*, 2 vols. (Wien and Teschen: Verlag der k. k. Hofbuchhandlung, 1884), II, 165-167.

108. Cf. Sammons, op. cit, p.90 for assimilative developments in Mendelssohn's family. Four of his six children converted, his daughter Dorothea married Friedrich Schlegel. Cf. also: Helmut Schanze: "Dorothea geb. Mendelssohn, Friedrich Schlegel, Philipp Veit—ein Kapitel zum Problem Judentum und Romantik," *Judentum, Antisemitismus und europäische Kultur*, Hans Otto Horch, ed. (Tübingen: A. Francke Verlag, 1988), pp.133-150.

109. For the relationship between Jäger Gracchus and Odradek, cf. Malcolm Pasley, "Two Kafka Enigmas: 'Elf Söhne' and 'Die Sorgen des Hausvaters'," *MLR*, 59 (1964), 73-81, 76 f.; "Die Sorge des Hausvaters," *Akzente*, 13 (1966), 303-309, 305 f.; "Kafka's Semi-Private Games," *Oxford German Studies*, 6 (1971/72), 112-131, 125 f.

110. Cf. a strikingly similar remark by Wittgenstein: "Der Jude muß im eigentlichen Sinn 'sein Sach' auf nichts stellen'. Aber das fällt gerade ihm besonders schwer, weil er, sozusagen, nichts hat." Wittgenstein, 1980, p.19.

111. Eggers, op. cit., vol.II, 350.

112. Cf. ibid., 358.

113. Cf. Eberhard Frey, "Der 'nüchtern-realistische, dialektisch doppelbödige' Stil Franz Kafkas," *Franz Kafka. Eine Aufsatzsammlung nach einem Symposium in Philadelphia*, ed. Maria Luise Caputo-Mayr, Schriftreihe Agora 29 (Berlin: Agora, 1978), 205-214, esp. 210 f., 212; for further sources, cf. Thieberger, op. cit., 189, 201.

114. Cf. Eggers, op. cit., II, 353 ff.; Blackall, op. cit., p.351, pp.482-526.

115. Eggers, op. cit., II, 357.

116. Cf. Israel Chalfen's marvelous biography *Paul Celan. Eine Biographie seiner Jugend* (Frankfurt/M: Insel Verlag, 1979).

117. I wish to thank Ralph Raico for pointing this out to me in a conversation.

118. Cf. also Thieberger, op. cit., 177 f.

119. Cf. Jörgen Kobs, *Kafka. Untersuchungen zu Bewußtsein und Sprache seiner Gestalten*, ed. Ursula Brech (Bad Homburg v.d.H.: Athenäum Verlag, 1970), p.107, 429; Thieberger, op. cit., 200 f.

120. Herman Hesse, *Neue deutsche Bücher. Literaturberichte für Bonniers "Litterära Magasin" 1935-1936*, ed. Bernhard Zeller (Marbach a.N.: Schiller-National Museum, 1965), pp. 8 f.; cf. Thieberger, op. cit., 179.

121. Mauthner, op. cit., p.49.

122. Cf. Thieberger, op. cit., 179.

123. Mauthner, op. cit., p.51.

124. Ibid.

125. J.W. Marchand in conversation.

126. Cf. also Gertrude Durusoy, *L'incidence de la littérature et de la langue tchèques sur les nouvelles de Franz Kafka* (Berne, Francfort/M: Peter Lang, 1981)

127. Cf. Binder "Kafkas Schaffensprozeß, mit besonderer Berücksichtigung des 'Urteils'. Eine Analyse seiner Aussagen über das Schreiben mit Hilfe der Handschriften und auf Grund psychologischer Theoreme," *Euphorion*, 70 (1976), 129-174, 143 f.; also: H.B., *Kafka. Der Schaffensprozeß* (Frankfurt/M: Suhrkamp, 1983), pp.29 ff.

128. E.g., Georg Büchner, who wrote a fragmentary *Novelle* about him, Paul Celan, who included his figure as a key symbol of the modern poet in his Georg-Büchner-Preis acceptance speech, or, more recently, Gert Hofmann, who wrote a continuation of Büchner's story. (Cf. Georg

Büchner, *Sämtliche Werke und Briefe. Historisch-kritische Ausgabe*, ed. Werner L. Lehmann, 2 vols. (München: Christian Wegner Verlag, 1974), I, 437-483; Paul Celan, *Gesammelte Werke in fünf Bänden* (Frankfurt/M: Suhrkamp, 1983), III, 187-202; Gert Hofmann, "Die Rückkehr des verlorenen Jakob Michael Reinhold Lenz nach Riga," G.H, *Gespräch über Balzacs Pferde. Vier Novellen* (Salzburg und Wien, 1981), pp.7-39. For the reception of Lenz in Germany, cf. Inge Stephan, Hans-Gerd Winter *Ein vorübergehender Meteor? J.M.R. Lenz und seine Rezeption in Deutschland* (Stuttgart: J.B. Metzlersche Verlagsbuchhandlung, 1984).

129. Cf. Kessler, op. cit., pp.1-4. Cf. also: Walter H. Sokel, "Von der Sprachkrise zu Kafkas Poetik," *Österreichische Gegenwart. Die moderne Literatur und ihr Verhältnis zur Tradition*, ed. Wolfgang Paulsen, Elftes Amherster Kolloquium zur deutschen Literatur (Bern und München: Francke Verlag 1980), pp.39-58, esp. pp.53 f.; Lukas Trabert, "Erkenntnis- und Sprachproblematik in Franz Kafkas *Beschreibung eines Kampfes* vor dem Hintergrund von Friedrich Nietzsches *Über Wahrheit und Lüge im außermoralischen Sinne*," DVS, 61 (1987), 298-324.

130. Cf. Dagmar Fischer, *Der Rätselcharakter der Dichtung Kafkas* (Frankfurt/M, Bern: Lang, 1985). For the debate on whether and how Kafka's stories can be understood, cf. Ingeborg C. Henel, "Die Deutbarkeit von Kafkas Werken," ZDP, 86 (1967), 250-266, rept. in: *Franz Kafka*, ed. Heinz Politzer, Wege der Forschung 322 (Darmstadt: Wissenschaftliche Buchgesellschaft, 1973), 406-430; Peter Heller, "On Not Understanding Kafka," *German Quarterly*, 47 (1974), 373-393; Christiaan L. Hart, "Die verschwiegene Botschaft oder: Bestimmte Interpretierbarkeit als Wirkungsbedingung von Kafkas Rätseltexten," DVS, 51

(1977), 459-475; Richard Bertelsmann, "Das verschleiernde Deuten. Kommunikation in Kafkas Erzählung 'Das Schweigen der Sirenen,'" *Acta Germanica,* 15 (1982), 63-75.

131. For the role of "right" and "wrong" in aesthetics, cf. Wittgenstein, "Lectures on Aesthetics," L.W., *Lectures and Conversations on Aesthetics, Psychology and Religious Belief,* compiled from notes taken by Yorrik Smythies, Rush Rhees and James Taylor, ed. Cyril Barrett (Berkeley and Los Angeles: University of California Press, 1966), pp.1-40, pp.4 ff.; B.R. Tilghman, "Aesthetics and the Complexity of Perception," B.R.T., *But Is It Art? The Value of Art and the Temptation of Theory* (Oxford: Basil Blackwell, 1984), pp. 122-151, esp. pp.149 ff.   Croce, too, denies that our relationship to art can be understood in terms of "conceptual knowledge" but, rather, must be regarded as a matter of "intuition" (Wittgenstein would have said, a matter of human reactions), a central concept in Croce's view on aesthetics. Cf. Benedetto Croce, *The Essence of Aesthetics,* tr. by Douglas Ainslie (London: William Heinemann, 1921), esp. pp.8, 16, 30.

132. Cf. Binder, "Kafka's literarische Urteile," *ZDP,* 86 (1967), 211-249, 226 ff.

133. Cf. ibid., 217f.

134. Cf. Pawel, op. cit., pp.110-114.

135. Cf. Dorothea Kuhn, "Versuch über Modelle in der Goethezeit," *Genius Huius Loci. Dank an Leiva Petersen,* ed. Dorothea Kuhn und Bernhard Zeller (Wien, Köln, Graz: Hermann Böhlaus Nachf., 1982), pp.267-290.

136. Cf. Kuhn, op. cit., David R. Stevenson, "Vico's *Scienza Nuova*: An Alternative to the Enlightenment Mainstream," *The Quest for the New Science: Language and Thought in Eighteenth-Century Science*, ed. by Karl J. Fink and J.W. Marchand (Carbondale and Edwardsville: Southern Illinois University Press, 1979), pp.6-16, esp. p.10.; K. Michael Seibt, "*Einfühlung*, Language and Herder's Philosophy of History," ibid., pp.17-27, esp. p.23, 26 f.

137. I wish to thank Bruce Goldberg for pointing out to me this trend in European *Geistesgeschichte*.

138. Cf. also Binder 1967, 231.

139. Gottfried Kölwel, *Prosa, Dramen, Verse*, ed. Ernst Alker, Rosa Kölwel und Peter Seufert, 3 vols. (München, Wien: Albert Langen, Georg Müller, 1964), III, 83.

140. Cf. also Binder "Schaffensprozeß" 1976, 142 f.

141. Cf. ibid., 145.

142. Ibid.

143. J.W. Marchand has drawn my attention to the fact that this title itself points toward Kafka's concern with the loss of roots, for it means literally someone who has lost contact with the soil.

144. While Tieck's device might be considered an expression of romantic irony, Brecht's similar technique (hopefully) serves the purpose of raising social consciousness. For romantic irony, cf. Ingrid Strohschneider-Kohrs, "Zur Poetik der deutschen Romantik II: Die romantische Ironie," *Die deutsche Romantik. Poetik, Formen und Motive*, ed. Hans Steffen (Göttingen: Vandenhoeck & Ruprecht, 1967), pp.75-

97. For Brecht's dramatic theory, cf. Bertolt Brecht, "Kritik der Einfühlung," B.B., *Gesammelte Werke in 20 Bänden*, ed. Elisabeth Hauptmann (Frankfurt/M: Suhrkamp Verlag, 1967), XV, 240-262; "Das epische Theater," ibid., 262-316; "Kleines Organon für das Theater," ibid., XVI, 661-709.

145. Cf. Tucholsky, "In der Strafkolonie," K.T., *Gesammelte Werke*, ed. Mary Gerold-Tucholsky, Fritz J. Raddatz, 4 vols. (Hamburg: Rowohlt Verlag, 1960-1962), I, 664-666, 666; Günther Anders, *Kafka Pro und Contra* (München: C.H. Beck'sche Verlagsbuchhandlung, 1951), pp.66 f.; Thieberger, op. cit., 201; Frey, op. cit., 210 f.; Kafka himself commented on the "cool" quality of his writing already in the *Kunstwart* days: " . . . mein Liebstes und Härtestes ist nur kühl . . . " (Br 19).

146. *Allgemeine Deutsche Biographie.* Neudruck der 1. Auflage von 1875 (Berlin: Duncker & Humblot, 1967).

147. Thieberger, op. cit., 180.

148. Fritz Mauthner, *Beiträge zu einer Kritik der Sprache*, 3 vols. (Stuttgart: Cotta, 1901-1902).

149. A veritable flood of literature has been written on the subject of "Sprachkrise" and "Sprachkritik" in European literature of the twentieth century. The following represents only a small selection of this literature. For the Austrian "Sprachkrise" around 1900, cf. Helmut Prang, "Der moderne Dichter und das arme Wort," *GRM*, 38 (1957), 130-145; Theodore Ziolkowski, "James Joyces Epiphanie und die Überwindung der empirischen Welt in der modernen deutschen Prosa," *DVS*, 35 (1961), 594-616; Wolfdietrich Rasch, "Aspekte der deutschen Literatur um 1900," W.R.

Zur deutschen Literatur seit der Jahrhundertwende. Gesammelte Aufsätze (Stuttgart: J.B. Metzlersche Verlagsbuchhandlung, 1967), pp.1-48; Fernand Hoffmann, "Sprachkrise als schöpferischer Impuls oder Wittgenstein und die Folgen," *Jahrbuch des Internationalen Dialekt-Instituts* (1979), 9-30; Richard T. Gray, "Aphorism and *Sprachkrise* in Turn-of-the Century Austria," *Orbis Litterarum*, 41 (1986), 332-354; further, two collections of essays: *Sprachthematik in der österreichischen Literatur des 20. Jahrhunderts*, ed. Institut für Österreichkunde (Wien: Verlag Ferdinand Hirt, 1974); *Thematisierung der Sprache in der österreichischen Literatur des 20. Jahrhunderts*, ed. Michael Klein and Sigurd Paul Scheichl, Innsbrucker Beiträge zur Kulturwissenschaft, Germanistische Reihe 7 (Innsbruck: Steigerdruck, 1982).

150. Another author associated with this conservative trend was Paul Ernst, whom Kafka met personally, commenting in his diary on Ernst's "contempt for our time" (T 662 ff.), and who had an important influence on Wittgenstein's concept of the "Mißverstehen der Sprachlogik." Cf. Ludwig Wittgenstein, "Bemerkungen über Frazers *The Golden Bough*," *Synthese*, 17 (1967), 233-253; Paul Ernst, "Nachwort," *Kinder- und Hausmärchen gesammelt durch die Brüder Grimm*, ed. P.E., 3 vols. (München and Leipzig: Georg Müller, 1910), III, 271-314, esp.273 f., 308; Rush Rhees, "Wittgenstein on Language and Ritual," *Acta Philosophica Fennica*, 28 (1976), issues 1-3, Essays on Wittgenstein in Honor of G.H. von Wright, 450-484, 456; Paul Hübscher, *Der Einfluß von Johann Wolfgang Goethe und Paul Ernst auf Ludwig Wittgenstein*, Europäische Hochschulschriften Reihe Philosophie, vol.185 (Bern, Frankfurt/M, New York: Peter Lang, 1985), 135-155.

151. Mauthner 1901, I, 181.

152. For a good discussion of this subject, cf. Jorn K. Bramann, "Religious Language in Wittgenstein and Kafka," *Diogenes* (Summer 1975), Nr.90, 26-35.

153. For a brief but excellent historical survey of the "Unsagbarkeittopos," cf. Bodo Müller, "Der Verlust der Sprache. Zur linguistischen Krise in der Literatur," *GRM*, N.F. 16 (1966), 225-243.

154. I wish to thank Randy Cooper for this very helpful and illuminating comment.

155. A good example of the application of such standards in matters of aesthetics is given in Wittgenstein's "Lectures on Aesthetics," where he discusses the use of words like "right" and "correct" in aesthetics. He compares this use to the way a tailor might judge the length of a coat. "'That's the right length,' 'That's too short,' 'That's too narrow'" (Wittgenstein 1966, p.5). Choosing a material for a coat, one might say: "'No. This is slightly too dark. This is slightly too loud' . . . . Similarly in music: 'Does this harmonize? No. The bass is not quite loud enough. Here I just want something different . . . '" (Ibid, p.7).

156. Cf. Peter Winch, "Language, Belief and Relativism," *Trying to Make Sense*, (Oxford: Basil Blackwell, 1987), pp.194-207, p.205.

157. Cf. Gershom G. Scholem, *Major Trends in Jewish Mysticism* (New York: Schocken Books, 1941), p.344; Martin Buber, *Hasidism* (New York: Philosophical Library, 1948), p.62; M.B., *The Origin and Meaning of Hasidism* (New York: Horizon Press, 1960), p.149; Harry M. Rabinowicz, *A Guide to Hassidism* (New York, London: Thomas Yoseloff, 1960), p.28; H.M.R., *The World of*

Hasidism (London: Valentine, Mitchell, 1970), p.183; and for a first-hand view: *Hasidic Anthology*, ed. Louis Newman (New York: Schocken Books, 1963).

158. For an account of the life of this remarkable woman, cf. Pawel, op. cit., pp.87 f., pp.349-352, 355.

159. Cf. Bezzel, op. cit., 129; Rotraut Hackermüller, *Das Leben das mich stört—Kafkas letzte Jahre* (Wien, Berlin: Medusa Verlag, 1984), pp. 28 ff.

160. Cf. Bezzel, op. cit., 130.

161. For Kafka's relationship to Kierkegaard's thought, cf. Ritchie Robertson, "Kafka's Zürauer Aphorisms," *Oxford German Studies*, 14 (1983), 73-91, 75-78; Wolfgang Lange, "Über Kafkas Kierkegaard-Lektüre und einige damit zusammenhängende Gegenstände," *DVS*, 60, 1986, 286-308.

162. For "court," cf. Rabinowizc, 1960, pp.89-101.

163. Cf. also Binder, "Kafka's Hebräischstudien," *Jb. d. DSG*, 11 (1967), 527-556.

164. Emmy L. Kerkhoff, "Noch einmal Franz Kafkas 'Von den Gleichnissen'. Vorgreifliche Bemerkungen zu einer Deutung," *Dichter und Leser*, ed. Ferdinand van Ingen et al. (Groningen: Wolters-Noordhoff, 1972), pp.191-195; Werner Hoffmann, *Kafkas Aphorismen* (Bern and München: Francke Verlag, 1975); Karl Erich Grözinger: "Himmlische Gerichte, Widergänger und Zwischenweltliche in der ostjüdischen Erzählung," *Kafka und das Judentum*, ed. K. E. G., Stéphan Mosès, Hans Dieter Zimmermann (Frankfurt/M: Jüdischer Verlag bei Athenäum, 1987), pp.93-112; Marina Cavarocchi Arbib, "Jüdische Motive in Kafkas Aphorismen," ibid., pp.122-146. This may be the best point to refer the reader

to additional literature concerning Kafka's relationship to Judaism. The great importance of this relationship has been ignored by the Kafka literature to a remarkable extent. As Pawel says, "What he was and what he did, cannot possibly be understood without a clear realization that his being Jewish . . . was at least as vital a component of his identity as his face or his voice." Pawel, op. cit., p.54. As early as 1931, Scholem commented on Kafka's affinity with traditional Judaism, especially the Book of Job. Cf. Stéphan Mosès, "Das Kafka-Bild Gershom Scholems," *Merkur*, 33 (1979), 862-867. For further discussions, cf. Charles Neider, "Franz Kafka and the Cabbalists," *Quarterly Review of Literature*, 2 (1945), 250-267; Baruch Kurzweil,"Die Fragwürdigkeit der jüdischen Existenz und das Problem der Sprachgestaltung," *Bulletin des Leo Baeck Instituts*, 8 (1965), 28-40; Werner Hoffmann, "Kafka und die jüdische Mystik," *Stimmen der Zeit*, 97 vol.190 (1972), 230-48; Hans Dieter Zimmermann, op. cit., pp.237-253; Harold Bloom, *The Strong Light of the Canonical: Kafka, Freud and Scholem as Revisionists of Jewish Culture*, City College Papers 20 (New York: Harold Bloom, 1987), 1-25.

165. Cf. Felix Weltsch, "Kafkas Aphorismen," *Neue Deutsche Hefte*, 1 (1954/55), 307-312; Günther Braun, "Franz Kafkas Aphorismen: Humoristische Meditation der Existenz," *Der Deutschunterricht*, 18 (1966), 107-118; for a survey of the literature on this subject, cf. Werner Hoffmann, 1975, pp.5-11; for more recent discussions, cf. Helen Milfull, "The Theological Position of Franz Kafka's Aphorisms," *Seminar*, 18 (1982), 169-83; Ritchie Robertson 1983, 73-91, esp. 82-89; Richard T. Gray, "Suggestive Metaphor: Kafka's Aphorisms and the Crisis of Communication," *DVS*, 58 (1984), 454-469; Werner Hoffmann, *'Ansturm gegen die letzte irdische Grenze'. Aphorismen und Spätwerk Kafkas* (Bern and München: Francke Verlag, 1984),

pp.11-24; Konrad Dietzfelbinger, *Kafkas Geheimnis. Eine Interpretation von Kafkas "Betrachtungen über Sünde, Leid, Hoffnung und den wahren Weg"* (Freiburg i. Br.: Aurum-Verlag, 1987).

166. cf. Rush Rhees, "Natural Theology," R.R., *Without Answers* (London: Routledge & Kegan Paul, 1969), pp.110-114.

167. Cf. Paul Engelmann, *Ludwig Wittgenstein. Briefe und Begegnungen*, ed. B.F. McGuinness (Wien and München: R.Oldenbourg, 1970), pp.101 f.

168. Cf. Rush Rhees, "Some Developments in Wittgenstein's View on Ethics," *Philosophical Review*, 74 (1965), 17-26, 21; Cora Diamond, "Wittgenstein, Ethics and the Psychology of Illusion" (manuscript).

169. Cf. Cora Diamond, op. cit.

170. Cf. Rhees, 1965, 19.

171. Friedrich Waismann, *Wittgenstein und der Wiener Kreis*, ed. B.F. McGuinness (Oxford: Basil Blackwell, 1967), p.117.

172. Waismann, op. cit., p.117.

173. Ibid.

174. Ibid.

175. Rhees, 1965.

176. Ibid., 19.

177. Ibid., 25.

178. Engelmann, op. cit., p.16.

179. Ibid., pp.6-17.

180. Rhees, 1965, 25.

181. Cf. Peter Winch, "Eine Einstellung zur Seele," P.W., 1987, pp.140-153, esp. p.148.

182. *Hasidic Anthology*, pp.125 f.

183. Ibid.

184. Ibid.

185. *In Praise of the Baal Shem Tov*, tr. and ed. Dan Ben-Amos and Jerome R. Mintz (Bloomington, London: Indiana University Press, 1977), pp.134 f.

186. Rather than listing the numerous discussions of this text, I will refer the reader to two such discussions, which contain comprehensive reviews of the secondary literature on this subject: Ingrid Strohschneider-Kohrs, "Erzähllogik und Verstehensprozeß in Kafka's Gleichnis 'Von den Gleichnissen'," *Probleme des Erzählens in der Weltliteratur*, ed. Fritz Martini (Stuttgart: Ernst Klett Verlag, 1971), pp.303-329, pp.304 ff.; Gerhard Buhr, "Franz Kafka, 'Von den Gleichnissen'. Versuch einer Deutung," *Euphorion*, 74 (1980), 169-185, esp. 169 f. and 182-185. For an interpretation that sees Kafka's parable as half Nietzschean, half deconstructionist, cf. Charles Bernheimer, "Crossing Over: Kafka's Metatextual Parable," *Modern Language Notes*, 95 (1980), 1254-1267. For a collection of essays on Kafka and parables, cf. *Die deutsche Parabel*, ed. Josef Billen, Wege

der Forschung 384 (Darmstadt: Wissenschaftliche Buchgesellschaft, 1986).   For a study of some of Kafka's other short
prose texts that might be called parables, cf. Peter Bekes,
Parabeln von Berthold Brecht, Franz Kafka, Günter Kunert
(Stuttgart: Ernst Klett Verlag, 1988), pp.10-26.

187. Cf. Bezzel, op. cit., 184.

188. Cf. Kessler, op. cit., pp.2 ff.

189. Kittler, op. cit., p.7.

190. Thorlby, op. cit., p. 69.

191. Pawel, 1984, p.355.

Bibliography

Primary Sources

Ben-Amos, Dan and Mintz, Jerome R., tr. & ed. *In Praise of the Baal Shem Tov*. Bloomington, London: Indiana University Press, 1977.

Brecht, Bertolt. *Gesammelte Werke in 20 Bänden*. Ed. Elisabeth Hauptmann. Frankfurt/M: Suhrkamp Verlag, 1967.

Brod, Max. *Streitbares Leben. Autobiographie*. München: Kindler, 1960.

Büchner, Georg. *Sämtliche Werke und Briefe. Historisch-kritische Ausgabe*. Ed. Werner L. Lehmann, 2 vols. München: Christian Wegner Verlag, 1974.

Busch, Wilhelm. *Historisch-kritische Gesamtausgabe*. Ed. Friedrich Bohne. 4 vols. Zürich: Stauffacher Verlag, 1959.

Celan, Paul. *Gesammelte Werke in fünf Bänden*. Frankfurt/M: Suhrkamp, 1983.

Ernst, Paul. "Nachwort," *Kinder- und Hausmärchen gesammelt durch die Brüder Grimm.* Ed. P.E. 3 vols. München und Leipzig: Georg Müller, 1910, III, 271-314.

Grimm, Jacob. *Über den Ursprung der Sprache.* Berlin: Ferdinand Dümmler's Verlagsbuchhandlung, 1858.

Hasidic Anthology. Ed. Louis Newman. New York: Schocken Books, 1963.

Heilmann, Hans. Tr. and ed. *Die Fruchtschale: Chinesische Lyrik vom 12. Jahrhundert vor Chr. bis zur Gegenwart.* Tr. and ed. Hans Heilmann. München & Leipzig: R. Piper & Co., 1905.

Heinrich Heines sämtliche Werke. Ed. Ernst Elster. 7 vols. Leipzig und Wien: Bibliographisches Institut, 1887-1890.

Herders sämtliche Werke. Ed. Bernhard Suphan. 33 vols. Berlin: Weidmann, 1877-1913.

Hofmann, Gert. *Gespräch über Balzacs Pferde. Vier Novellen.* Salzburg und Wien, 1981.

Hofmannsthal, Hugo von. "Ein Brief." H.v.H. *Gesammelte Werke in Einzelausgaben. Prosa*, 3 vols. Ed. Herbert Steiner. II, 7-20.

Humboldt, Wilhelm von. *Werke in fünf Bänden.* Ed. Andreas Flitner and Klaus Giel. Stuttgart: J.G. Cotta'sche Buchhandlung, 1963.

Janouch, Gustav. *Gespräche mit Kafka. Aufzeichnungen und Erinnerungen.* Erweiterte Ausgabe. Frankfurt/M: S. Fischer Verlag, 1968.

Kafka, Franz. *Tagebücher und Briefe*. Gesammelte Schriften, VI. Ed. Max Brod. Prag: Verlag Heinr. Mercy Sohn, 1937.

——— *Erzählungen und kleine Prosa*. Gesammelte Schriften, I. Ed. Max Brod. New York: Schocken Books, 1946.

——— *Beschreibung eines Kampfes. Novellen, Skizzen, Aphorismen aus dem Nachlaß*. Gesammelte Schriften, V. Ed. Max Brod. New York: Schocken Books, 1946.

——— *Tagebücher 1910-1923*. Gesammelte Werke. Ed. Max Brod. Frankfurt/M: S. Fischer Verlag, 1948.

The Diaries of Franz Kafka. Tr. Joseph Kresh. 2 vols. New York: Schocken Books, 1948.

——— *Briefe an Milena*. Ed. Willy Haas. Gesammelte Werke. Ed. Max Brod. Frankfurt/M: S. Fischer Verlag, 1952.

——— *Hochzeitsvorbereitungen auf dem Lande und andere Prosa aus dem Nachlaß*. Gesammelte Werke. Ed. Max Brod. Frankfurt/M: S. Fischer Verlag, 1953.

——— *Briefe 1902-1924*. Gesammelte Werke. Ed. Max Brod. Frankfurt/M: S. Fischer Verlag, 1958.

——— *Die Erzählungen*. Frankfurt/M: S. Fischer Verlag, 1961.

——— *Die Romane. Amerika. Der Prozeß. Das Schloß*. Frankfurt/M: S. Fischer Verlag, 1966.

——— *Briefe an Felice und andere Korrespondenz aus der*

Verlobungszeit. Ed. Erich Heller and Jürgen Born. Gesammelte Werke. Ed. Max Brod. Frankfurt/M: S. Fischer Verlag, 1967.

———— *Beschreibung eines Kampfes. Die zwei Fassungen. Parallelausgabe nach den Handschriften.* Ed. Max Brod. Text ed. Ludwig Dietz. Frankfurt/M: S. Fischer Verlag, 1969.

———— *Briefe an Ottla und die Familie.* Ed. Hartmut Binder and Klaus Wagenbach. Gesammelte Werke. Frankfurt/M: S.Fischer Verlag, 1974.

———— *"Das Urteil." Text, Materialien, Kommentar.* Ed. Gerhard Neumann. Literatur-Kommentare, XVI. Ed. Hans-Joachim Simm et al. München, Wien: Carl Hanser Verlag, 1981.

———— *Das Schloß.* Ed. Malcolm Pasley. Kritische Ausgabe. Ed. Jürgen Born et al. 2 vols. Frankfurt/M: S. Fischer, 1982.

———— *Der Verschollene.* Ed. Jost Schillemeit. Kritische Ausgabe. Ed. Jürgen Born et al. 2 vols. Frankfurt/M: S. Fischer, 1983.

———— *Amtliche Schriften.* Ed. Klaus Hermsdorf. Berlin: Akademie Verlag, 1984.

Kölwel, Gottfried. *Prosa, Dramen, Verse.* Ed. Ernst Alker, Rosa Kölwel and Peter Seufert. 3 vols. München, Wien: Albert Langen, Georg Müller, 1964.

Kraus, Karl. *Werke.* Ed. Heinrich Fischer. 14 vols. München: Kösel Verlag, 1954-1967.

Langer, Georg M. *Neun Tore. Das Geheimnis der Chassidim.* Tr. Dr.Friedrich Thieberger. Introd. Gershom Scholem. München-Planegg: O.W. Barth, 1959.

Liliencron, Detlev von. *Gesammelte Werke.* Ed. Richard Dehmel. 8 vols. Berlin: Schuster & Löeffler, 1911.

Mann, Thomas. *Ausgewählte Erzählungen.* Stockholm: Bermann-Fischer Verlag, 1948.

Mauthner, Fritz. *Beiträge zu einer Kritik der Sprache.* 3 vols. Stuttgart: Cotta, 1901-1902.

———— *Prager Jugendjahre.* Frankfurt/M: S. Fischer Verlag, 1969.

Max Brod, Franz Kafka. Eine Freundschaft. Reiseaufzeichnungen. Ed. Malcolm Pasley, Hannelore Rodlauer. Frankfurt/M: S. Fischer Verlag, 1987.

Meißner, Alfred. *Geschichte meines Lebens.* 2 vols. Wien and Teschen: Verlag der k. k. Hofbuchhandlung, 1884.

Mendelssohn, Moses. *Gesammelte Schriften.* Ed. I.Elbogen, Alexander Altmann. 19 vols. Stuttgart, Bad Cannstadt: Friedrich Frommann Verlag, 1971-74.

Schoeps, Julius H., ed. *Im Streit um Kafka und das Judentum. Max Brod. Hans-Joachim Schoeps. Briefwechsel.* Königstein/Ts: Jüdischer Verlag bei Athenäum, 1985.

Singer, Isaac Bashevis. *A Friend of Kafka and Other Stories,* New York: Farrar, Straus and Giroux, 1970.

Storm, Theodor. *Sämtliche Werke.* Ed. Albert Köster. 8 vols.

Leipzig: Insel, 1919-20.

Tucholsky, Kurt. *Gesammelte Werke*. Ed. Mary Gerold-Tucholsky, Fritz J. Raddatz. 4 vols. Hamburg: Rowohlt Verlag, 1960-1962.

—— *Ausgewählte Briefe*. Hamburg: Rowohlt Verlag, 1960.

Wittgenstein, Ludwig. *Tractatus Logico-Philosophicus. Logisch-philosophische Abhandlung*. Tr. D.F. Pears & B.F. McGuinness, with an introduction by Bertrand Russell. London: Routledge & Kegan Paul, 1961.

—— *Philosophical Investigations. Philosophische Untersuchungen*. Tr. G.E.M. Anscombe. New York: The Macmillan Company, 1953.

—— *The Blue and Brown Books. Preliminary Studies for the Philosophical Investigations*. New York, Cambridge: Harper & Row, 1958.

—— *Notebooks 1914-1916*. Ed. G.H. von Wright and G.E.M. Anscombe, tr. G.E.M. Anscombe. Oxford: University of Chicago Press, 1961.

—— *Philosophische Bemerkungen*. Ed. Rush Rhees. Oxford: Basil Blackwell, 1964.

—— "Wittgenstein's Lecture on Ethics." *Philosophical Review* 74 (1965), 3-12.

—— "Lectures on Aesthetics," L.W., *Lectures and Conversations on Aesthetics, Psychology and Religious Belief*. Compiled from notes taken by Yorrik Smythies, Rush Rhees and James Taylor. Ed. Cyril Barrett.

Berkeley and Los Angeles: University of California Press, 1966.

───── "Bemerkungen über Frazers *The Golden Bough.*" *Synthese* 17 (1967), 233-253.

───── *Zettel.* Ed. G.E.M. Ascombe and G.H. von Wright, tr. G.E.M. A. Oxford: Basil Blackwell, 1967.

───── *Philosophische Grammatik.* Ed. Rush Rhees. Oxford: Basil Blackwell, 1969.

───── *On Certainty. Über Gewißheit.* Ed. G.E.M. Anscombe & G.H. von Wright, tr. Denis Paul and G.E.M. Anscombe. New York, London: Harper & Row, 1969.

───── *Briefe an Ludwig von Ficker.* Ed. Georg von Wright. *Brenner Studien* 1. Salzburg: Otto Müller Verlag, 1969.

───── *Bemerkungen über die Grundlagen der Mathematik.* Ed. G.E.M. Anscombe, Rush Rhees and G.H. von Wright. Revidierte und erweiterte Ausgabe. *Schriften* VI. Frankfurt/M: Suhrkamp Verlag, 1974.

───── *Remarks on the Philosophy of Psychology. Bemerkungen über die Philosophie der Psychologie.* Ed. G.H. von Wright and Heikki Nyman, tr. C.G. Luckhardt and M.A.E. Aue. 2 vols. Oxford: University of Chicago Press, 1980.

───── *Culture and Value.* Ed. G.H. von Wright, tr. Peter Winch. Chicago: University of Chicago Press, 1980.

───── *Last Writings on the Philosophy of Psychology. Letzte Bemerkungen über die Philosophie der Psychologie.* Ed.

G.H. von Wright and Heikki Nyman, tr. C.G. Luckhardt and Maximilian A.E. Aue. Oxford: The University of Chicago Press, 1982.

Bibliographies and Reference Works

Allgemeine Deutsche Biographie. Neudruck der 1. Aufl. von 1875. Berlin: Duncker & Humblot, 1967.

Caputo-Mayr, Maria Luise and Julius M. Herz. *Franz Kafkas Werke. Eine Bibliographie der Primärliteratur*. Bern und München: Francke Verlag, 1982.

———— et al. Franz Kafka. *Eine kommentierte Bibliographie der Sekundärliteratur 1955-1980, mit einem Nachtrag 1985*. Bern und Stuttgart: Francke Verlag, 1987.

Dietz, Ludwig. *Franz Kafka. Die Veröffentlichungen zu seinen Lebzeiten (1908-1924). Eine textkritische und kommentierte Bibliographie*. Repertoria Heidelbergensia IV. Heidelberg: Lothar Stiehm Verlag, 1982.

Ducrot, Oswald, Tzvetan Todorov. *Dictionnaire encyclopédique des sciences du langage*. Paris: Éditions du Seuil, 1972.

Encyclopaedia Judaica. Jerusalem, Israel: Keter Publishing House Ltd., 1971.

German Jewry: Its History, Life and Culture. Ed. Ilse R. Wolff. The Wiener Library Catalogue Series No.3. London: Vallentine, Mitchell, 1958.

Kayser, Werner and Horst Gronemeyer. *Max Brod.* Hamburger Bibliographien 12. Hamburg: Hans Christian Verlag, 1972.

Kisch, Guido. *Judaistische Bibliographie. Ein Verzeichnis der in Deutschland und der Schweiz von 1956 bis 1970 erschienen Dissertationen und Habilitationsschriften.* Basel, Stuttgart: Helbig & Lichtenhahn, 1972.

Muneles, Otto. *Bibliografický Prehled Zidoské Prahy.* Státni Zidoské Museum v Praze, 1952.

Shunami, Shlomo. *Bibliography of Jewish Bibiliographies.* Jerusalem: The Magnes Press, The Hebrew University, 1965.

Weinreich, Uriel and Beatrice. *Yiddish Language and Folklore: A Selective Bibliography for Research.* S'Gravenhage: Mouton & Co., 1959.

Secondary Sources

Allemann, Beda. "Der Prozeß." *Der deutsche Roman.* Vol.II. Ed. Benno von Wiese. Düsseldorf: August Bagel Verlag, 1965, 234-290.

—— "Kafka. Von den Gleichnissen." *ZDP* 83 (1964), 97-106.

Alt, Peter-André. "Doppelte Schrift, Unterbrechung und Grenze." *Jb.d.DSG* 29 (1985), 455-490.

Altmann, Alexander. *Moses Mendelssohn: A Biographical Study*. University: University of Alabama Press, 1973.

—— *Essays in Jewish Intellectual History*. Hanover, New Hampshire & London: Brandeis University Press, 1981.

Anders, Günther. *Kafka Pro und Contra*. München: C.H. Beck'sche Verlagsbuchhandlung, 1951.

Apel, Karl Otto. *Die Idee der Sprache in der Tradition des Humanismus von Dante bis Vico*. Archiv für Begriffsgeschichte, Bausteine zu einem historischen Wörterbuch der Philosophie, VIII. Bonn: H.Bouvier u. Co. Verlag, 1963.

Arbib, Marina Cavarocchi. "Jüdische Motive in Kafkas Aphorismen." *Kafka und das Judentum*. Ed. Karl Erich Grözinger, Stéphan Mosès, Hans Dieter Zimmermann. Frankfurt/M: Jüdischer Verlag bei Athenäum, 1987, pp.122-146.

Arntzen, Helmut. "Franz Kafka. Von den Gleichnissen." *ZDP* 83 (1964), 106-113.

—— "Franz Kafka. Der Prozeß." H.A.: *Der moderne deutsche Roman*. Heidelberg: Wolfgang Rothe Verlag, 1962, pp.76-100.

Backenköhler, Gerd. "Neues zum 'Sorgenkind Odradek'." *ZDP* 89 (1970), 269-273.

Ball, Patricia. "Sincerity: The Rise and Fall of a Critical Term." *MLR* 19 (1964), 1-11.

Bansberg, Dietger. "Durch Lüge zur Wahrheit. Eine Inter-

170   *Gabriele von Natzmer Cooper*

vaters'." *ZDP* 93 (1974), 257-269.

Barner, Wilfried. "Vorurteil, Empirie, Rettung. Der junge
Lessing und die Juden." *Juden und Judentum in der
Literatur.* Ed. Herbert A. Strauss and Christhard
Hoffmann. München: Deutscher Taschenbuch Verlag,
1985. pp.52-77.

Barnouw, Dagmar. "Loos, Kraus, Wittgenstein and the
Problem of Authenticity." *The Turn of the Century:
German Literature and Art 1890-1915.* Ed. Gerald
Chapple and Hans H. Schulte. The McMaster Colloquium
on German Literature. Bonn: Bouvier Verlag, 1981.
pp.249-273

Baum, Alwin L. "Parable as Paradox in Kafka's Erzählungen." *Modern Language Notes* 91 (1976), 1327-1347.

Beck, Evelyn Torton. *Kafka and the Yiddish Theater: Its
Impact on His Work.* Madison, Milwaukee and London:
The University of Wisconsin Press, 1971.

Bekes, Peter. *Parabeln von Berthold Brecht, Franz Kafka,
Günter Kunert.* Stuttgart: Ernst Klett Verlag, 1988.

Benjamin, Walter. "Franz Kafka. Zur Wiederkehr seines
Todestages." *Benjamin über Kafka. Texte, Briefzeugnisse,
Aufzeichnungen.* Ed. Hermann Schweppenhäuser. Frank-
furt/M: Suhrkamp Verlag, 1981, pp.9-38.

Ben-Sasson, H.H., ed. *A History of the Jewish People.*
Cambridge, Mass.: Harvard University Press, 1976.

Bense, Max. *Die Theorie Kafkas.* Köln, Berlin: Kiepenheuer

& Witsch, 1952.

Benzmann, Hans. "Die Entwicklung der modernen deutschen Lyrik." *Moderne deutsche Lyrik*. Ed. H.B. Leipzig: P. Reclam jun., 1924. pp.5-56.

Ben-Zvi, Linda. "Samuel Beckett, Fritz Mauthner, and the Limits of Language." *PMLA* 95 (1980), 183-200.

Berg, Leo. "Detlev von Liliencron und die moderne Lyrik." *Das Magazin für Literatur*, 69 (1900), Nr.50, col.1241-1244 and Nr. 51, col.1269. Rept. *Literarische Manifeste der Jahrhundertwende. 1890-1910*. Ed. Erich Ruprecht & Dieter Bänsch. Stuttgart: J.B. Metzlersche Verlagsbuchhandlung, 1970. pp.72-76.

Bernheimer, Charles. "Crossing Over: Kafka's Metatextual Parable." *Modern Language Notes* 95 (1980), 1254-1267.

Bertelsmann, Richard. "Das verschleiernde Deuten. Kommunikation in Kafkas Erzählung 'Das Schweigen der Sirenen.'" *Acto Germanica* 15 (1982), 63-75.

Bezzel, Chris. *Kafka Chronik*. Reihe Hanser 178. München-Wien: Hanser Verlag, 1975.

Bieber, Hugo. "Jews and Jewish Problems in German Literature." *The Jewish People Past and Present*. Ed. Salo W. Baron et al. 4 vols. New York: Jewish Encyclopedic Handbooks, Central Yiddish Culture Organization (CYCO), 1952, III, 239-256.

Billen, Josef, ed. *Die deutsche Parabel*. Wege der Forschung 384. Darmstadt: Wissenschaftliche Buchgesellschaft, 1986.

Binder, Hartmut. *Motiv und Gestaltung bei Franz Kafka.* Abhandlungen zur Kunst-, Musik- und Literaturwissenschaft, XXXVII. Bonn: H.Bouvier u. Co. Verlag, 1966.

―――― "Kafkas Hebräischstudien. Ein biographisch-interpretatorischer Versuch." *Jb.d. DSG* 11 (1967), 527- 556.

―――― "Kafkas literarische Urteile. Ein Beitrag zu seiner Typologie und Ästhetik." *ZDP* 86 (1967), 211-249.

―――― "'Der Jäger Gracchus.' Zu Kafkas Schaffensweise und poetischer Topographie." *Jb.d.DSG* 15 (1971), 375-440.

―――― *Kafka Kommentar zu sämtlichen Erzählungen.* München: Winkler Verlag, 1975.

―――― *Kafka in neuer Sicht.* Stuttgart: J.B. Metzler, 1976.

―――― "Kafkas Schaffensprozeß, mit besonderer Berücksichtigung des 'Urteils'. Eine Analyse seiner Aussagen über das Schreiben mit Hilfe der Handschriften und auf Grund psychologischer Theoreme." *Euphorion* 70 (1976), 129-174.

―――― *Kafka-Kommentar zu den Romanen, Rezensionen, Aphorismen und zum Brief an den Vater.* München: Winkler Verlag, 1976.

―――― *Franz Kafka. Leben und Persönlichkeit.* Stuttgart: Alfred Kröner Verlag, 1979.

―――― *Kafka. Ein Leben in Prag.* München: Mahnert-Lueg, 1982.

—— *Kafka. Der Schaffensprozeß*. Frankfurt/M: Suhrkamp, 1983.

Birnbaum, S.A. *Yiddish: A Survey and a Grammar*. Toronto, Buffalo: University of Toronto Press, 1979.

Blackall, Eric. *The Emergence of German as a Literary Language*. Cambridge: University Press, 1959.

Bloch, Chajim. *Die Gemeinde der Chassidim: Ihr Werden und ihre Lehre*. Berlin: Harz, 1920.

Bloom, Harold. *The Strong Light of the Canonical: Kafka, Freud and Scholem as Revisionists of Jewish Culture*. City College Papers 20. New York: Harold Bloom, 1987.

Böckel, Fritz. *Detlev von Liliencron. Erinnerungen und Urteile*. Second, enlarged ed. of *Liliencron im Urteil zeitgenössischer Dichter*. 2. Sonderheft der *Xenien. Monatsschrift für Literatur und Kunst*. Leipzig: Xenien-Verlag, 1912.

Böhle, Rüdiger E. "Der Begriff der Sprache bei Wilhelm von Humboldt und Ludwig Wittgenstein." *Dimensionen der Sprache in der Philosophie des deutschen Idealismus. Bruno Liebrucks zum 70. Geburtstag zugeeignet*. Ed. Brigitte Scheer und Günter Wohlfahrt. Würzburg: Königshausen & Neumann, 1982, pp.190- 213.

Born, Jürgen. "Franz Kafka und Felice Bauer. Ihre Beziehung im Spiegel des Briefwechsels 1912-1917." *ZDP* 86 (1967), 176-196.

—— "Das Feuer zusammenhängender Stunden. Zu Kafkas Metaphorik des dichterischen Schaffens." *Nachleben der*

Romantik in der modernen deutschen Literatur. Die Vorträge des zweiten Kolloquiums in Amherst, Mass. Ed. Wolfgang Paulsen. Heidelberg: Lothar Stiehm Verlag, 1969, pp.177-191.

Borries, Mechthild. *Ein Angriff auf Heinrich Heine. Kritische Betrachtungen zu Karl Kraus.* Studien zur Poetik und Geschichte der Literatur, 13. Stuttgart, Berlin, Köln, Mainz: Verlag W. Kohlhammer, 1971.

Bramann, Jorn K. "Religious Language in Wittgenstein and Kafka." *Diogenes* (Summer 1975), Nr.90, 26-35.

Braun, Günther. "Franz Kafkas Aphorismen. Humoristische Meditation der Existenz." *Der Deutschunterricht* 18 (1966), 107-118.

Brod, Max. "Der Dichter Franz Kafka." *Juden in der deutschen Literatur.* Ed. Gustav Krojanker. Berlin: Welt Verlag, 1922, pp.55-62.

——— "Ein Brief an den Vater." *Der Monat* 8/9 (1949), 98-105.

——— "Keine Flickarbeit. Eine Erinnerung an Franz Kafka anläßlich seines fünfundzwanzigsten Todestages im Juni 1949." *Berliner Hefte* 4 (1949), 7-9.

——— *Verzweiflung und Erlösung im Werk Franz Kafkas.* Frankfurt/M: S.Fischer Verlag, 1959.

——— *Franz Kafka. Eine Biographie.* New York: Schocken Books,1954, rept. Frankfurt/M: Fischer Verlag, 1962.

——— "Aus Kafkas Freundeskreis." *Wort in der Zeit* 10

(1964), 4-6.

—— *Der Prager Kreis*. Stuttgart, Berlin, Köln, Mainz: W.Kohlhammer Verlag, 1966.

—— *Franz Kafkas Glauben und Lehre*. M. B. *Über Franz Kafka*. Frankfurt/M: Fischer Bücherei, 1966, pp.223-302.

Brosch, Leonhard. *Kafka und Prag*. Pfullingen: Verlag Günther Neske, 1983.

Buber, Martin. *Hasidism*. New York: Philosophical Library, 1948.

—— *The Origin and Meaning of Hasidism*. New York: Horizon Press, 1960.

Buhr, Gerhard. "Franz Kafka, 'Von den Gleichnissen'. Versuch einer Deutung." *Euphorion* 74 (1980), 169-185.

Canetti, Elias. *Der andere Prozeß. Kafkas Briefe an Felice*. Reihe Hanser, XXIII. München: Carl Hanser Verlag, 1970.

Chalfen, Israel. *Paul Celan. Eine Biographie seiner Jugend*. Frankfurt/M: Insel Verlag, 1979.

Conditio Judaica. *Judentum, Antisemitismus und deutschsprachige Literatur vom 18. Jahrhundert bis zum Ersten Weltkrieg*. Vol.1. Ed. Hans Otto Horch und Horst Denkler. Tübingen: Max Niemeyer Verlag, 1988.

Cooper, Gabriele. "Tanzende Chiffren: Heines Faust." *Maske und Kothurn* 12 (1986), 41-52.

Coseriu, Eugenio. *Die Geschichte der Sprachphilosophie von der Antike bis zur Gegenwart. Eine Übersicht.* 2 vols. Tübinger Beiträge zur Linguistik, XI, XXVIII. Ed. Gunter Narr. Tübingen: Tübinger Beiträge zur Linguistik, 1970, 1972.

Croce, Benedetto. *The Essence of Aesthetics.* Tr. by Douglas Ainslie. London: William Heinemann, 1921.

David, Annie. *Von den Juden in Deutschland 1600-1870. Ein Bildbericht.* Jerusalem: Massada Press, 1973.

Dawidowicz, Lucy. *The War against the Jews.* London: Weidenfeld and Nicolson, 1975.

Demetz, Peter. "Noch einmal: Prager Deutsch." *Literatur und Kritik* 6 (1966), 58-59.

Dietz, Ludwig. "Franz Kafka und die Zweimonatsschrift *Hyperion.* Ein Beitrag zur Biographie, Bibliographie und Datierung seiner frühen Prosa." *DVS* 37 (1963), 463-473.

———— "Franz Kafka. Drucke zu seinen Lebzeiten. Eine textkritisch-biibliographische Studie." *Jb.d.DSG* 7 (1963), 416-457.

———— "Die autorisierten Dichtungen Kafkas. Textkritische Anmerkungen." *ZDP* 86 (1967), 301-317.

———— "Kafkas Randstriche in Manuskript B der 'Beschreibung eines Kampfes' und ihre Deutung. Eine Ergänzung zu der zweiten Fassung." *Jb.d.DSG* 16 (1972), 648-658.

———— "Max Brods Hand in Kafkas Manuskripten der 'Beschreibung eines Kampfes' und seine Kontamination dieser Novelle. Ein Beitrag zur Textgeschichte und Textkritik." *GRM* 23 (1973), 187-197.

—— "Die Datierung von Kafkas 'Beschreibung eines Kampfes' und ihrer vollständigen Handschrift." *Jb.d.DSG* 17 (1973), 490-503.

—— "Editionsprobleme bei Kafka. Über einen kritischen Text der 'Beschreibung eines Kampfes." *Jb.d.DSG* 18 (1974), 549- 558.

—— *Franz Kafka.* Sammlung Metzler, Realien zur Literatur, Abt. D: Literaturgeschichte. Stuttgart: J.B. Metzlersche Verlagsbuchhandlung, 1975.

Dietzfelbinger, Konrad. *Kafkas Geheimnis. Eine Interpretation von Kafkas "Betrachtungen über Sünde, Leid, Hoffnung und den wahren Weg."* Freiburg i. Br.: Aurum-Verlag, 1987.

Dubnow, Simon. *Weltgeschichte des Jüdischen Volkes von seinen Uranfängen bis zur Gegenwart in zehn Bänden.* Berlin: Jüdischer Verlag, 1923-1929.

Durusoy, Gertrude. *L'incidence de la littérature et de la langue tchèques sur les nouvelles de Franz Kafka.* Berne, Francfort/M: Peter Lang, 1981.

Edel, Edmund. "Zum Problem des Künstlers bei Kafka." *Der Deutschunterricht* 15 (1963), 9-31.

Edschmid, Kasimir. *Die doppelköpfige Nymphe.* Berlin: Paul Cassirer, 1920.

Eggers, Hans. *Deutsche Sprachgeschichte*. 2 vols. Hamburg: Rowohlts Enzyklopädie, 1986.

Eisner, Pavel. *Franz Kafka and Prague*. New York: Golden Griffin Books, 1950.

Elbogen, Ismar, Eleonore Sterlin. *Die Geschichte der Juden in Deutschland. Eine Einführung*. Bibliotheca Judaica. Frankfurt/M: Europäische Verlagsanstalt, 1966.

Emrich, Wilhelm. *Franz Kafka*. Bonn: Athenäum-Verlag, 1958.

———— "Die Sorge des Hausvaters." *Akzente* 13 (1966), 295-303.

Engelmann, Paul. *Ludwig Wittgenstein. Briefe und Begegnungen*. Ed. B.F. McGuinness. Wien und München: R. Oldenbourg, 1970.

Engler, R. *Théorie et Critique d'un principle saussurien, l'arbitraire du signe*. Genève: Cahiers Ferdinand de Saussure, vol. 19, 1962.

Eschenbacher, Walter. *Fritz Mauthner und die deutsche Literatur um 1900*. Frankfurt/M: Peter Lang, 1977.

Fickert, Kurt. "Symbol and Myth. Kafka's 'A Father's Concern'." *Germanic Notes* 6 (1975), 59-62.

Fischer, Dagmar. *Der Rätselcharakter der Dichtung Kafkas*. Frankfurt/M, Bern: Lang, 1985.

Frey, Eberhard. "Der 'nüchtern-realistische, dialektisch doppelbödige' Stil Franz Kafkas." *Franz Kafka. Eine Aufsatz-*

sammlung nach einem Symposium in Philadelphia. Ed. Maria Luise Caputo-Mayr. Schriftreihe Agora 29. Berlin: Agora, 1978, 205-214.

Geiger, Ludwig. *Die deutsche Literatur und die Juden.* Berlin: Georg Reimer, 1910.

Gerhard, Marlis. *Die Sprache Kafkas. Eine semiotische Untersuchung.* Diss. Stuttgart, 1969.

Gerzon, Jacob. *Die jüdisch-deutsche Sprache. Eine grammatikalisch-lexikalische Untersuchung ihres deutschen Grundbestandes.* Frankfurt/M: J. Kauffmann, 1902.

Graetz, H. *Volkstümliche Geschichte der Juden.* 3 vols., Leipzig: O. Leiner 1888-89, rept. Berlin, Wien: Benjamin Harz Verlag, 1922.

Graupe, Heinz Mosche. *Die Entstehung des modernen Judentums. Geistesgeschichte der deutschen Juden 1650-1942.* Hamburg: Leibniz-Verlag, 1969.

Gray, Richard T. "Suggestive Metaphor: Kafka's Aphorisms and the Crisis of Communication." *DVS* 58 (1984), 454-469.

——— "Aphorism and *Sprachkrise* in Turn-of-the Century Austria." *Orbis Litterarum* 41 (1986), 332-354.

Grözinger, Karl Erich. "Die hassidische Erzählung, ihre Formen und Traditionen." *Frankfurter Judaistische Beiträge* 9 (1981), 91-114.

——— "Himmlische Gerichte, Widergänger und Zwischenweltliche in der ostjüdischen Erzählung." *Kafka und das*

Judentum. Ed. K. E. G., Stéphan Mosès, Hans Dieter Zimmermann. Frankfurt/M: Jüdischer Verlag bei Athenäum, 1987, pp.93-112.

Gruša, Jiří. *Franz Kafka of Prague.* Tr. Eric Mosbacher. New York: Schocken Books, 1983.

Haas, Willy. "Geheimnisse des alten Prag." W.H.: *Die literarische Welt. Erinnerungen.* München: Paul List Verlag, 1957, pp.9-39.

—— "Das Unvergessene." *Wort in der Zeit* 10 (1964), 8-10.

Hackermüller, Rotraut. *Das Leben das mich stört—Kafkas letzte Jahre.* Wien, Berlin: Medusa Verlag, 1984.

Hardt, Ludwig. "Erinnerung an Franz Kafka." *Neue Rundschau* 58 (1947), 239-242.

Hart Nibbrig, Christiaan L. "Die verschwiegene Botschaft oder: Bestimmte Interpretierbarkeit als Wirkungsbedingung von Kafkas Rätseltexten." *DVS* 51 (1977), 459-475.

Hart, Julius. "Die Entwicklung der neueren Lyrik in Deutschland." *Pan* 4 (1896), Nr.1, 33-40. Rept. *Literarische Manifeste der Jahrhundertwende. 1890-1910.* Ed. Erich Ruprecht & Dieter Bänsch. Stuttgart: J.B. Metzlersche Verlagsbuchhandlung, 1970, pp.5-23.

Hasselblatt, Dieter. *Zauber und Logik. Eine Kafka-Studie.* Köln: Verlag Wissenschaft und Politik, 1964.

Havránek, Bohuslav. "The Functional Differentiation of the Standard Language." *A Prague School Reader on Aesthet-*

ics, Literary Structure, and Style. Ed. and tr. from the original Czech by Paul L. Garvin. Washington, D.C.: Georgetown University Press, 1964, pp.13-16.

Heintz, Günter. *Franz Kafka. Sprachreflexion als dichterische Einbildungskraft.* Würzburg: Königshausen & Neumann, 1983.

Heller, Peter. "On Not Understanding Kafka." *German Quarterly* 47 (1974), 373-393.

Henel, Ingeborg C. "Die Deutbarkeit von Kafkas Werken." *ZDP* 86 (1967), 250-266. Rept. in *Franz Kafka.* Wege der Forschung 322. Darmstadt: Wissenschaftliche Buchgesellschaft, 1973, 406-430.

Hering, Gerhard F. "Franz Kafkas Tagebücher." *Merkur* 2 (1948), 96-109.

Hermsdorf, Klaus. "Zu den Briefen Franz Kafkas." *Sinn und Form* 9 (1957), 653-662.

————— "Künstler und Kunst bei Franz Kafka." *Weimarer Beiträge* 10 (1964), 404-412.

Hertzberger, Arthur. *The Zionist Idea: A Historical Analysis and Reader.* Garden City, N.Y.: Doubleday & Co., Inc. and Herzl Press, 1959.

Herz, Julius M. "Franz Kafka and Austria: National Background and Ethnic Identity." *Modern Austrian Literature* 11 no. 3/4 (1978), 301-318.

Hess, Moses. *Rome and Jerusalem: A Study in Jewish Nationalism.* Tr. Meyer Waxman. New York: Bloch Publishing Co., 1943.

Hesse, Hermann. *Neue deutsche Bücher. Literaturberichte für Bonniers "Litterära Magasin" 1935-1936.* Ed. Bernhard Zeller. Marbach a.N.: Schiller-National Museum, 1965, pp.8-9, 26-27.

Hiebel, Hans H. "Antihermeneutik und Exegese. Kafkas ästhetische Figur der Unbestimmtheit." *DVS* 52 (1978), 90-110.

Hillmann, Heinz. *Franz Kafka. Dichtungstheorie und Dichtungsgestalt.* Bonner Arbeiten zur deutschen Literatur, IX. Ed. Benno von Wiese. Bonn: H. Bouvier u. Co. Verlag, 1964.

—— "Das Sorgenkind Odradek." *ZDP* 86 (1967), 197-210.

Hodin, J.P. "Erinnerungen an Franz Kafka." *Der Monat* 1 (1949), 89-96.

Hoffmann, Fernand. "Sprachkrise als schöpferischer Impuls oder Wittgenstein und die Folgen." *Jahrbuch des Internationalen Dialekt-Instituts* (1979), 9-30.

Hoffmann, Werner. "Kafka und die jüdische Mystik." *Stimmen der Zeit* 97, vol.190 (1972), 230-48.

—— *Kafkas Aphorismen.* Bern and München: Francke Verlag, 1975.

—— *'Ansturm gegen die letzte irdische Grenze'. Aphorismen und Spätwerk Kafkas.* Bern and München: Francke Verlag, 1984.

Höllerer, Walter. "Odradek unter der Stiege." Eröffnungs-referat für das Franz-Kafka-Symposium London, 20.10. 1983. *Sprache im technischen Zeitalter* (1983), 350-362.

Hornschuh, Manfred. *Die Tagebücher Franz Kafkas. Funktionen, Formen, Kontraste.* Frankfurt/M, Bern: Lang, 1987.

Hübscher, Paul. *Der Einfluß von Johann Wolfgang Goethe und Paul Ernst auf Ludwig Wittgenstein.* Europäische Hochschulschriften, Reihe Philosophie, vol.185. Bern, Frankfurt/M, New York: Peter Lang, 1985.

Im Zeichen Hiobs. Jüdische Schriftsteller und deutsche Literatur im 20. Jahrhundert. Ed. Gunter E. Grimm, Hans-Peter Bayerdörfer. Königstein/Ts.: Athenäum Verlag 1985.

Jackson, Wallace. *Immediacy: The Development of a Critical Concept from Addison to Coleridge.* Amsterdam: Rodopi 1973.

Jacobi, Ruth L. *Heines jüdisches Erbe.* Bonn: Bouvier Verlag Herbert Grundmann, 1978.

Jahn, Wolfgang. "Kafka und die Anfänge des Kinos." *Jb. d. DSG* 6 (1962), 353-368.

Jenaczek, Friedrich. *Zeittafeln zur "Fackel". Themen, Ziele, Probleme.* München: Kösel Verlag, 1965.

Juden in der deutschen Literatur. Essays über zeitgenössische Schriftsteller. Berlin: Welt Verlag, 1922.

Juden in der deutschen Literatur. Ein deutsch-israelisches

Symposium. Ed. Albrecht Schöne. Frankfurt/M: Suhrkamp Verlag, 1983.

Kerkhoff, Emmy L. "Noch einmal Franz Kafkas 'Von den Gleichnissen.' Vorgreifliche Bemerkungen zu einer Deutung." *Dichter und Leser.* Ed. Ferdinand van Ingen et al. Groningen: Wolters-Noordhoff, 1972, pp.191-195.

Kessler, Susanne. *Kafka—Poetik der sinnlichen Welt.* Stuttgart: J.B. Metzlersche Verlagsbuchhandlung, 1983.

Kircher, Hartmut. *Heinrich Heine und das Judentum.* Bonn: Bouvier Verlag Herbert Grundmann, 1973.

Kisch, Egon. *Die Abenteuer in Prag.* Wien, Prag, Leipzig: Verlag Ed. Strache, 1920.

——— *Vom Marktplatz der Sensationen.* London: Verlag Jugend Voran, 1943. *Marktplatz der Sensationen.* New ed. Berlin: Aufbau Verlag, 1949.

Kisch, Guido. *Die Prager Universität und die Juden 1348-1848. Mit Beiträgen zur Geschichte des Medizinstudiums.* Amsterdam: Verlag B.R. Grüner, 1935.

Kittler, Wolf. *Der Turmbau zu Babel und das Schweigen der Sirenen. Über das Reden, das Schweigen, die Stimme und die Schrift in vier Texten von Franz Kafka.* Erlangen: Verlag Palme & Enke, 1985.

Klein, Michael and Scheichl, Sigurd Paul, ed. *Thematisierung der Sprache in der österreichischen Literatur des 20. Jahrhunderts.* Innsbrucker Beiträge zur Kulturwissenschaft, Germanistische Reihe 7. Innsbruck: Steigerdruck, 1982.

Kobs, Jörgen. *Kafka. Untersuchungen zu Bewußtsein und Sprache seiner Gestalten.* Ed. Ursula Brech. Bad Homburg v.d.H.: Athenäum Verlag, 1970.

Koch, Hans-Gerd. "Chronik zum jungen Kafka im Umkreis des kulturellen Lebens von Prag." *Der junge Kafka.* Ed. Gerhard Kurz. Frankfurt/M: Suhrkamp, 1984, pp.242-252.

Koelb, Clayton. *Kafka's Rhetoric: The Passion of Reading.* Ithaca and London: Cornell University Press, 1989.

Kohn, Caroline. *Karl Kraus.* Stuttgart: J.B. Metzlersche Verlagsbuchhandlung, 1966.

Kraft, Werner. *Karl Kraus. Beiträge zum Verständnis seines Werkes.* Salzburg: Otto Müller Verlag, 1956.

Krčmář, Dr. Jan. *The Prague Universities. Compiled According to the Sources and Records.* Prague: Orbis Press, 1934.

Kremer, Detlef. *Die Erotik des Schreibens.* Frankfurt/M: Athenäum, 1989.

Kuepper, Karl J. "Gesture and Posture as Elemental Symbolism in Kafka's *The Trial.*" *Mosaic* 3 (1969/70), 143-152.

Kuhn, Dorothea. "Versuch über Modelle in der Goethezeit." *Genius Huius Loci. Dank an Leiva Petersen.* Ed. Dorothea Kuhn und Bernhard Zeller. Wien, Köln, Graz: Hermann Böhlaus Nachf., 1982, pp.267-290.

Kühn, Joachim. *Gescheiterte Sprachkritik.* Berlin, New York:

Walter de Gruyter, 1975.

Kühne, Jörg. *"Wie das Rascheln in den gefallenen Blättern."
Versuch zu Franz Kafka.* Tübingen-Bebenhause: Verlag
Lothar Rotsch, 1975.

Kurz, Gerhard. "Schnörkel und Schleier und Warzen. Die
Briefe Kafkas an Oskar Pollak und seine literarischen
Anfänge." *Der junge Kafka.* Ed. Gerhard Kurz. Frank-
furt/M: Suhrkamp, 1984, pp.68-101.

Kurzweil, Baruch. "Die Fragwürdigkeit der jüdischen Existenz und das Problem der Sprachgestaltung." *Bulletin des
Leo Baeck Instituts* 8 (1965), 28-40.

———— "Franz Kafka: Jüdische Existenz ohne Glauben." *Die
Neue Rundschau* (1966), 418-436.

Lange, Wolfgang. "Über Kafkas Kierkegaard-Lektüre und
einige damit zusammmenhängende Gegenstände," *DVS*
60 (1986), 286-308.

Leinfellner, Elisabeth. "Zur nominalistischen Begründung
von Linguistik und Sprachphilosophie: Fritz Mauthner
und Ludwig Wittgenstein." *Studium Generale* 22 (1969),
209-251.

Lifson, David S. *The Yiddish Theater in America.* New York,
London: Thomas Yoseloff, 1965.

Liptzin, Sol. *A History of Yiddish Literature.* Middle Village,
N.Y.: Jonathan David Publishers, 1972.

———— *Flowering of Yiddish Literature* New York, London:
Thomas Yoseloff, 1963.

Loewe, Heinrich. *Die jüdisch-deutsche Sprache der Ostjuden. Ein Abriß im Auftrag des "Komitees für den Osten."* Berlin, 1915.

Lublinski, Samuel. *Die Entstehung des Judentums. Eine Skizze.* Berlin: Jüdischer Verlag, 1903.

Malcolm, Norman. *Ludwig Wittgenstein. A Memoir and a Biographical Sketch by W.H. von Wright.* 2nd ed. Oxford, New York: Oxford University Press, 1984.

Mann, Klaus. *Der Wendepunkt.* Frankfurt/M, 1952, pp.347, 428-429, 454, 476-477.

Marchand, James W. "Herder: Precursor of Humboldt, Whorf and Modern Language Philosophy." *Johann Gottfried Herder: Innovator through the Ages.* Ed. Wulf Koepke in cooperation with Samson B. Knoll. Modern German Series, 10. Bonn: Bouvier, 1982, 20-34.

—— "Proto Yiddish and the Glosses: Can We Reconstruct Proto Yiddish?" *Origins of the Yiddish Language.* Winter Studies in Yiddish, vol I. Papers from the First Annual Oxford Winter Symposium in Yiddish Language and Literature, 15-17 December 1985. Ed. Dovid Katz. Oxford: Pergamon Press, 1987, 83-94.

—— "Goethes 'Judenpredigt'," *Monatshefte* 50 (1958), 305-310.

Margetts, John. "Satzsyntaktisches Spiel mit der Sprache. Zu Franz Kafkas 'Auf der Galerie'." *Colloquia Germanica* 4 (1970), 76-82.

Mayo, Bruce. "Interpreting Kafka's Hidden Laughter." *Ger-*

manic Review 53 (1978), 166-173.

Michels, Gerd. "Scheiternde Mimesis. Zu Franz Kafka: 'Die Sorge des Hausvaters'." *Festschrift für Friedrich Kienecker.* Ed. Gerd Michels. Heidelberg, 1980, pp.179-198.

Milfull, Helen. "The Theological Position of Franz Kafka's Aphorisms." *Seminar* 18 (1982), 169-83.

Mosès, Stéphan. "Das Kafka-Bild Gershom Scholems." *Merkur* 33 (1979), 862-67.

Mukařovský, Jan. "Standard Language and Poetic Language." *A Prague School Reader on Aesthetics, Literary Structure, and Style.* Ed. and tr. from the original Czech by Paul L. Garvin. Washington, D.C.: Georgetown University Press, 1964, pp.17-30.

Müller, Bodo. "Der Verlust der Sprache. Zur linguistischen Krise in der Literatur." *GRM* N.F. 16 (1966), 225-243.

Muschg, Walter. "Kafka. Der Künstler." W.M.: *Gestalten und Figuren.* Bern und München: Francke Verlag, 1968, pp.103-126.

Neider, Charles. "Franz Kafka and the Cabbalists." *Quarterly Review of Literature* 2 (1945), 250-267.

Neumann, Gerhard. "Die Arbeit im Alchimistengäßchen." *Kafka- Handbuch.* Ed. Hartmut Binder. 2 vols. Stuttgart: Alfred Kröner Verlag, 1979, II, 313-349.

Nicolai, Ralf N. "Diskussionsbeitrag zu Kafkas 'Die Sorge des Hausvaters'." *Revue des langues vivantes* 41 (1975), 156-161.

Nutting, Peter West. "Kafka's 'strahlende Heiterkeit': Discursive Humor and Comic Narration in *Das Schloß*." *DVS* 57 (1983), 651-78.

Pasley, Malcolm. "Franz Kafka MSS. Description and Select Inedita." *MLR* 57 (1962), 53-59.

────── "Two Kafka Enigmas: 'Elf Söhne' and 'Die Sorge des Hausvaters'." *MLR* 59 (1964), 73-81.

────── "Die Sorge des Hausvaters." *Akzente* 13 (1966), 303-309.

────── "Kafka's Semi-Private Games." *Oxford German Studies* 6 (1971/72), 112-131.

Pawel, Ernst. *The Nightmare of Reason: A Life of Franz Kafka*. New York: Random House, 1984.

────── "Kafkas Judentum." *Kafka und das Judentum*. Ed. Karl Erich Grözer, Stéphan Mosès, Hans Dieter Zimmermann. Frankfurt/M: Jüdischer Verlag bei Athenäum, 1987, pp.253-258.

Philippi, Klaus-Peter. "Parabolisches Erzählen. Anmerkungen zu Form und möglicher Geschichte." *DVS* 43 (1969), 297-332.

Pierre, Rolland. *Odradek Loi de Kafka*. Paris: Les Éditeurs Français Réunis, 1976.

Pinès, M. *Histoire de la littérature judéo-allemande*. Paris: Jouve et Cie, 1911.

Politzer, Heinz. "Problematik und Probleme der Kafka-Forschung." *Monatshefte* 42 (1950), 273-280. Also: *Franz Kafka.* Ed. Heinz Politzer. Wege der Forschung 322. Darmstadt: Wissenschaftliche Buchgesellschaft, 1973, 214-225.

―――― "Prague and the Origins of Rainer Maria Rilke, Franz Kafka, and Franz Werfel." *Modern Language Quarterly* 16 (1955), 49-62.

―――― "Eine Parabel Franz Kafkas." *Jb.d.DSG* 4 (1960), 463- 483.

―――― *Franz Kafka, der Künstler.* Frankfurt/M: S.Fischer Verlag, 1962.

―――― "Das Schweigen der Sirenen." *DVS* 41 (1967), 444-467.

―――― "Zur Kafka-Philologie." *Franz Kafka.* Ed. H. Politzer. Wege der Forschung 322. Darmstadt: Wissenschaftliche Buchgesellschaft, 1973, 159-161.

―――― "Dieses Mütterchen hat Krallen." *Literatur und Kritik* 9 (1974), 15-33.

Pott, Hans-Georg. "Allegorie und Sprachverlust. Zu Kafkas *Hungerkünstler*-Zyklus und der Idee einer 'Kleinen Literatur'." *Euphorion* 73 (1979), 435-450.

Prang, Helmut. "Der moderne Dichter und das arme Wort." *GRM* 38 (1957), 130-145.

Prawer, S.S. *Heine's Jewish Comedy.* Oxford: Clarendon Press, 1983.

Raabe, Paul. "Franz Kafka und der Expressionismus." *ZDP* 86 (1967), 161-175. Rept. *Franz Kafka*. Ed. Heinz Politzer. Wege der Forschung 322. Darmstadt: Wissenschaftliche Buchgesellschaft, 1973, 386-405.

Rabinowicz, Harry M. *A Guide to Hassidism*. New York, London: Thomas Yoseloff, 1960.

—— *The World of Hasidism*. London: Valentine, Mitchell, 1970.

Rajek, Elisabeth M. *Namen und ihre Bedeutung im Werke Franz Kafkas. Ein interpretischer Versuch*. Europäische Hochschulschriften, Reihe I. Vol. 186. Bern, Frankfurt/M, Las Vegas: Peter Lang, 1977.

Rasch, Wolfdietrich. *Zur deutschen Literatur seit der Jahrhundertwende. Gesammelte Aufsätze*. Stuttgart: J.B. Metzlersche Verlagsbuchhandlung, 1967.

Reiss, Hans. "Kafka on the Writer's Task." *MLR* 66 (1971), 113-124.

Reissner, H.G. "Begegnung zwischen Deutschen und Juden im Zeichen der Romantik." *Das Judentum in der deutschen Umwelt 1800-1850*. Ed. Hans Liebeschütz und Arnold Paucker. Tübingen: J.C.B. Mohr (Paul Siebeck), 1977, pp.325-358.

Rey, Jean-Michel. *Quelqu'un danse. Les noms de F. Kafka*. Lille: Presses Universitaires de Lille, 1985.

Rhees, Rush. "Some Developments in Wittgenstein's View on Ethics." *Philosophical Review* 74 (1965), 17-26.

────── *Without Answers.* London: Routledge & Kegan Paul, 1969.

────── "Wittgenstein on Language and Ritual." *Acta Philosophica Fennica* 28 (1976), issues 1-3. Essays on Wittgenstein in Honor of G.H. von Wright, 450-484.

Roback, A.A. *The Story of Yiddish Literature.* New York: Yiddish Scientific Institute, 1940.

Robert, Marthe. "Dora Dymants Erinnerungen an Kafka." *Merkur* 7 (1953), 848-851.

Robertson, Ritchie. "Kafka's Zürauer Aphorisms." *Oxford German Studies* 14 (1983), 73-91.

────── *Kafka: Judaism, Politics and Literature.* Oxford: Clarendon Press, 1985.

Rolleston, James. "Das Frühwerk." *Kafka Handbuch.* Ed. Hartmut Binder. 2 vols. Stuttgart: Alfred Kröner Verlag, 1979, II, 242-261.

Roth, Cecil. *A Short History of the Jewish People.* Revised and enlarged illustrated edition. London: East and West Library, 1948.

Sammons, Jeffrey L. *Heinrich Heine: A Modern Biography.* Princeton, N.J.: Princeton University Press, 1979.

Sandrow, Nahma. *Vagabond Stars: A World History of Yiddish Theater.* New York: Seth Press, 1977

Saße, Günter. *Sprache und Kritik. Untersuchung zur Sprachkritik der Moderne.* Palaestra Band 267. Göttingen:

Vandenhoeck & Ruprecht, 1977.

—— "Die Sorge des Lesers. Zu Kafkas Erzählung 'Die Sorge des Hausvaters'." *Poetica* 10 (1978), 262-284.

Schanze, Helmut. "Dorothea geb. Mendelssohn, Friedrich Schlegel, Philipp Veit—ein Kapitel zum Problem Judentum und Romantik." *Judentum, Antisemitismus und europäische Kultur.* Ed. Hans Otto Horch. Tübingen: Francke Verlag, 1988, pp.133-150.

Schaub, Ute. "Liliencron und Heine im Urteil von Karl Kraus." *Heine Jahrbuch* 18 (1979), 191-201.

Schillemeit, Jost. "Zum Wirklichkeitsproblem der Kafka-Interpretation." *DVS* 40 (1966), 577-596.

—— "Kafkas 'Beschreibung eines Kampfes'. Ein Beitrag zum Textverständnis und zur Geschichte von Kafkas Schreiben." *Der junge Kafka.* Ed. Gerhard Kurz. Frankfurt/M: Suhrkamp, 1984, pp.102-132.

Schoeps, Hans Joachim. "Franz Kafka oder der Glaube in der tragischen Position." H.J.Sch.: *Gestalten an der Zeitwende.* Frankfurt/M: Atharva-Verlag, 1948, pp.51-68.

Scholem, Gershom G. *Major Trends in Jewish Mysticism.* New York: Schocken Books, 1941.

—— *Origins of the Kabbalah.* Ed. R.J. Werblowsky. Tr. from the German by Allan Arkush. The Jewish Publication Society, Princeton University, 1962.

—— *On the Kabbalah and Its Symbolism.* Tr. Ralph Manheim. New York: Schocken Books, 1965.

—— *Kabbalah.* Jerusalem, Israel: Quadrangle/The New York Times Book Co., 1974.

Seibt, K. Michael. *"Einfühlung,* Language and Herder's Philosophy of History." *The Quest for the New Science: Language and Thought in Eighteenth-Century Science.* Ed. Karl J. Fink and J.W. Marchand. Carbondale and Edwardsville: Southern Illinois University Press, 1979, pp.17-27.

Skala, Emil. "Das Prager Deutsch." *Zeitschrift für deutsche Sprache* 22 (1966), 84-91.

Smith, David E. *Gesture as a Stylistic Device in Kleist's "Michael Kohlhaas" and Kafka's "Der Prozess."* Stanford German Studies, 11. Bern: Herbert Lang, 1976.

Sokel, Walter H. *Franz Kafka. Tragik und Ironie.* München, Wien: Albert Langen, Georg Müller, 1964.

—— "Das Verhältnis der Erzählperspektive zu Erzählgeschehen und Sinngehalt in 'Vor dem Gesetz', 'Schakale und Araber' und 'Der Prozeß'." *ZDP* 86 (1967), 267-300.

—— "Von der Sprachkrise zu Kafkas Poetik." *Österreichische Gegenwart. Die moderne Literatur und ihr Verhältnis zur Tradition.* Ed. Wolfgang Paulsen. Bern, München: Francke, 1980, pp.39-58.

Spiero, Heinrich. *Detlev von Liliencron. Sein Leben und seine Werke.* Berlin & Leipzig: Schuster & Loeffler, 1913.

Sprachthematik in der österreichischen Literatur des 20. Jahrhunderts. Ed. Institut für Österreichkunde. Wien: Verlag

Ferdinand Hirt, 1974.

Stahl, August. "Konfusion ohne Absicht? Zur Interpretation von Kafkas Erzählung 'Die Sorge des Hausvaters'." *Saarbrücker Beiträge zur Ästhetik*. Ed. Rudolf Malter and Alois Brandstetter. Saarbrücken: Kommissionsverlag Buchhandlung der Saarbrücker Zeitung, 1966, pp.67-78.

Steinherz, Samuel. *Die Juden in Prag. Bilder aus ihrer tausendjährigen Geschichte. Festgabe der Logo Praga des Ordens B'nai B'rith zum Gedenktage ihres 25jährigen Bestandes*. Prag: Selbstverlag, 1927.

Steinschneider, Moritz. *Jewish Literature: From the Eighth to the Eighteenth Century with an Introduction on Talmud and Midrash. A Historical Essay*. Hildesheim: Georg Olms Verlagsbuchhandlung, 1967.

Stephan, Inge, Hans-Gerd Winter. *Ein vorübergehender Meteor? J.M.R. Lenz und seine Rezeption in Deutschland*. Stuttgart: J.B. Metzlersche Verlagsbuchhandlung, 1984.

Stern, J.P. "Franz Kafka on Mice and Men." *Literary Theory and Criticism: Festschrift Presented to René Wellek in Honor of his Eightieth Birthday*. Ed. Joseph P. Strelka. 2 vols. Bern, Frankfurt/M, 1985, II, 1297-1312.

Stern, Martin. "Der Briefwechsel Hofmannsthal—Fritz Mauthner." *Hofmannsthal Blätter* (1978), H. 19/20, 21-39.

Stevenson, David R. "Vico's *Scienza Nuova*: An Alternative to the Enlightenment Mainstream." *The Quest for the New Science: Language and Thought in Eighteenth-Century Science*. Ed. Karl J. Fink and J.W. Marchand. Carbondale and Edwardsville: Southern Illinois University Press, 1979, pp.6-16.

Stieg, Gerald. "Kafka als Spiegel der Kraus'schen Literaturpolemik." *Kontroversen, alte und neue.* Ed. Franz Josef Worstbrock. Tübingen: Niemeyer, 1986, pp.98-106.

Stölzl, Christoph. *Kafkas böses Böhmen. Zur Sozialgeschichte eines Prager Juden.* München: Text und Kritik, 1975.

Strohschneider-Kohrs, Ingrid. "Zur Poetik der deutschen Romantik II: Die romantische Ironie," *Die deutsche Romantik. Poetik, Formen und Motive.* Ed. Hans Steffen. Göttingen: Vandenhoeck & Ruprecht, 1967, pp.75-97.

——— "Erzähllogik und Verstehensprozeß in Kafkas Gleichnis 'Von den Gleichnissen'." *Probleme des Erzählens in der Weltliteratur.* Ed. Fritz Martini. Stuttgart: Ernst Klett Verlag, 1971, pp.303-329.

Susskind, N. "How Yiddish Originated." *Judah A. Joffe Book.* Ed. Yudel Mark. New York: Yivo Institute for Jewish Research, 1958, pp.146-157.

——— "A Partisan History of Yiddish." *Origins of the Yiddish Language.* Winter Studies in Yiddish, vol I. Papers from the First Annual Oxford Winter Symposium in Yiddish Language and Literature, 15-17 December 1985. Ed. Dovid Katz. Oxford: Pergamon Press, 1987, 127-134.

Teweles, Heinrich. *Kampf um die Sprache.* Leipzig: C. Reissner, 1884.

Thieberger, Richard. "Sprache," *Kafka-Handbuch*. Ed. Hartmut Binder. 2 vols. Stuttgart: Alfred Kröner Verlag, 1979, II, 177-203.

Thorlby, Anthony. "Anti-Mimesis: Kafka and Wittgenstein." *On Kafka*. Ed. Franz Kuna. London: Barnes & Noble Books, 1976, pp.59-82.

—— "Kafka and Language." *The World of Franz Kafka*. Ed. J.P. Stern. New York: Holt, Rinehart and Winston, 1980, pp.133-144.

Tilghman, B.R. *But Is It Art? The Value of Art and the Temptation of Theory*. Oxford: Basil Blackwell, 1984.

Trabert, Lukas. "Erkenntnis- und Sprachproblematik in Franz Kafkas 'Beschreibung eines Kampfes' vor dem Hintergrund von Friedrich Nietzsches *Über Wahrheit und Lüge im außermoralischen Sinne*." *DVS* 61 (1987), 298-324.

Tramer, Hans. "Prague—City of Three Peoples,"*Leo Baeck Institute Yearbook* 9 (1964), 305-339.

Triffit, Gregory B. *Kafka's 'Landarzt' Collection. Rhetoric and Interpretation*. Australia and New Zealand Studies in German Language and Literature. Vol.13. New York, Bern, Frankfurt/M.: Peter Lang, 1985.

Trilling, Lionel. *Sincerity and Authenticity*. Cambridge, Mass.: Harvard University Press, 1972.

Trost, Pavel. "Das späte Prager Deutsch." *Germanistica Pragensia* 2 (1962), 31-39.

Turk, Horst. "Die Wirklichkeit der Gleichnisse. Überlegungen zum Problem der objektiven Interpretation am Beispiel Kafkas." *Poetica* 8 (1976), 208-225.

Unseld, Joachim. "Franz Kafka. Die Privatisierung der Schriftstellerexistenz (1922-1924)." *Sprache im technischen Zeitalter* (1981), 291-310.

Urzidil, Gertrude. "My Personal Meetings with Franz Kafka." *Journal of Modern Literature* 6 (1977), 446-447.

Urzidil, Johannes. "Begegnungen mit Franz Kafka," *Neue Literarische Welt* No.2 (Jan. 25, 1952), 3.

—— "Kafkas Bestattung und Totenfeier." *Merkur* 18 (1964), 595-599.

—— "Edison und Kafka." *Der Monat* 13 (1960/61), 53-57.

—— "Von Odkolek zu Odradek." *Schweizer Monatshefte* 50 (1970/71), 957-972.

Wagenbach, Klaus. *Franz Kafka Eine Biographie seiner Jugend 1883-1912*. Bern: Francke Verlag, 1958.

—— *Franz Kafka in Selbstzeugnissen und Bilddokumenten*. Hamburg: Rowohlt Taschenbuch Verlag, 1964.

—— *Franz Kafka. Bilder aus seinem Leben*. Berlin: Verlag Klaus Wagenbach, 1983. Erweiterte und veränderte Neuausgabe, 1989.

Waismann, Friedrich. *Wittgenstein und der Wiener Kreis*. Ed. B.F. McGuinness. Oxford: Basil Blackwell, 1967.

Waxman, Meyer. *A History of Jewish Literature from the Close of the Bible to Our Own Days*. 4 vols. New York: Bloch Publishing Co., 1936.

Weiler, Gershon. *Mauthner's Critique of Language*. Cambridge: University Press, 1970.

Weinberg, Kurt. "Franz Kafkas 'Erste Veröffentlichung'." *ZDP* 81 (1962), 496-500.

Weinreich, Max. *History of the Yiddish Language*. Chicago and London: University of Chicago Press, 1973.

—— "Outlines of Western Yiddish." *Juda A. Joffe Book*, ed. Yudel Mark, New York: Yivo Institute for Jewish Research, 1958, pp.158-194.

Weinreich, Uriel. *College Yiddish: An Introduction to the Yiddish Language and to Jewish Life and Culture*. New York: Yiddish Scientific Institute—Yivo, second revised edition, 1953.

Weiss, Ernst. "Bemerkungen zu den Tagebüchern und Briefen Franz Kafkas." *Maß und Wert* 1 (1937/8), 319-325.

Weltsch, Felix. "Kafkas Aphorismen." *Neue Deutsche Hefte* 1 (1954/55), 307-312.

—— *Religion und Humor im Leben und Werk Franz Kafkas*. Berlin-Grunewald: F.A. Herbig Verlagsbuchhandlung, 1957.

—— "The Rise and Fall of the Jewish-German Symbiosis—the Case of Franz Kafka." *Leo Baeck Institute*

Yearbook 1 (1959), 255-276.

Wiener, Leo. *The History of Yiddish Literature in the Nineteenth Century.* London: John C. Nimmo, 1899.

Winch, Peter. *Trying to Make Sense.* Oxford: Basil Blackwell, 1987.

Winner, Thomas G. "Literature as a Semiotic System: The Case of Kafka's 'Metamorphosis' as a Metasemiotic Text." *Literary Theory and Criticism: Festschrift Presented to René Wellek in Honor off his Eightieth Birthday.* Ed. Joseph P. Strelka. Vol.I. Bern, Frankfurt/M, New York: Peter Lang, 1985, 657-676.

Zborowski, Mark and Margaret Mead. *Life is With the People. The Jewish Little-Town of Eastern Europe.* New York: International University Press, 1952.

Zimmermann, Hans Dieter. "Franz Kafka und das Judentum." *Juden und Judentum in der Literatur.* Ed. Herbert A. Strauss und Christhard Hoffmann. München: Deutscher Taschenbuch Verlag, 1985, pp.237-253.

Zinberg, Israel. *A History of Jewish Literature.* Tr. and ed. Bernhard Martin. 12 vols. New York: KTAV Publishing House, Inc., 1972-78.

Ziolkowski, Theodore. "James Joyces Epiphanie und die Überwindung der empirischen Welt in der modernen deutschen Prosa." *DVS* 35 (1961), 594-616.

Index

ARIADNE PRESS

Studies in Austrian Literature, Culture, and Thought

*Major Figures of
Modern Austrian Literature*
Edited by Donald G. Daviau

*Major Figures of
Turn-of-the-Century
Austrian Literature*
Edited by Donald G. Daviau

*Introducing Austria
A Short History*
By Lonnie Johnson

*Austrian Foreign Policy
Yearbook*
Report of the Austrian Federal
Ministry for Foreign Affairs
for the Year 1988

*The Verbal and Visual Art of
Alfred Kubin*
By Phillip H. Rhein

From Wilson to Waldheim
Proceedings of a Workshop on
Austrian-American Relations
1917-1987
Edited by Peter Pabisch

Arthur Schnitzler and Politics
By Adrian Clive Roberts

*Austria in the Thirties
Culture and Politics*
Edited by Kenneth Segar
and John Warren

*Stefan Zweig
An International Bibliography*
By Randolph J. Klawiter

*"What People Call Pessimism":
Sigmund Freud, Arthur Schnitzler
and Nineteenth-Century
Controversy at the University of
Vienna Medical School*
By Mark Luprecht

Quietude and Quest
Protagonists and Antagonists in
the Theatre, on and off Stage
As Seen through the Eyes of
Leon Askin
Written by Leon Askin with
C. Melvin Davidson

*Coexistent Contradictions
Joseph Roth in Retrospect*
Edited by Helen Chambers

*Kafka and Language
In the Stream of
Thoughts and Life*
By G. von Natzmer Cooper

Translation Series: